Audi

R8

www.veloce.co.uk

First published in August 2011 by Veloce Publishing Limited, Veloce House, Parkway Farm Business Park, Poundbury, Dorchester, Dorset DT1 3AR, England. Fax 01305 268864/e-mail info@veloce.co.uk/web www.veloce.co.uk or www.velocebooks.com. ISBN: 978-1-845843-27-4 UPC: 6-36847-04327-8
Readers with ideas for automotive books, or books on other transport or related hobby subjects, are invited to write to the editorial director of Veloce Publishing at the above address.
British Library Cataloguing in Publication Data – A catalogue record for this book is available from the British Library. Typesetting, design and page make-up all by Veloce Publishing Ltd on Apple Mac. Printed in India by Replika Press.

Audi

R8

VELOCE

WSC GIANTS™

Ian Wagstaff

Contents

Acknowledgements

Watching the four Audis at Le Mans in 1999, I was not quite sure what to make of them. I had seen Audis in the forests and in the snow, and that seemed to be their natural habitat. Yet here they were rounding Mulsanne corner, seeming to be interlopers in a race that was surely all about Toyota, BMW, and Mercedes-Benz. It took just 12 months to show that Audi was anything but an intruder. Looking back now, over the past decade, Audi has *been* Le Mans.

Its highly efficient media operation has eased the path of journalists throughout this period, and I must first thank Jon Zammet's UK team, including motorsport specialists Martin and Teresa Pass, as well as Kate Dixon and Robin Davies, for its assistance in the preparation of this book. In particular, I must single out David Ingram, once team manager of the Audi Sport UK racing operation, who is now part of that press operation as Public Relations Manager, Product and Technology; it is perhaps his enthusiasm, allied to Allan McNish's spirited driving, that has most contributed to any bias the British may now have towards this German marque.

There are others to whom I must also express my thanks for their help. Thirty-five drivers have competed with the Audi R8 at international level, a number of whom have shared their feelings for the car. In particular, I would like to thank that supreme trio, Allan McNish, Tom Kristensen, and Dindo Capello – whose win at Le Mans in 2008 was one of the defining moments of the decade, albeit in a diesel R10 – and also Andy Wallace, for giving their thoughts on the R8 specifically for this book. Sitting, listening to the enthusiastic Scot for an hour-or-so as he extolled the car's virtues, was a particular pleasure. My apologies to Finlay for monopolising his father. The men at Audi are also highly approachable and, in particular, I must single out Dr Wolfgang Ullrich and Ulrich Baretzky. Designer, Tony Southgate, was also particularly helpful, and is now featured in my third book running. Spending time at Brad Kettler's operation in Indiana not only taught me more about how Audi blitzed North America, but showed how Audi R8s (and I do not mean the GT R8s) are still racing there today; a fact not always realised in Europe. More than anybody, Brad continues to keep the R8 alive and is a joy to talk to about the car.

For the majority of the photos shot in the USA, I have to thank Gary Horrocks, Martin Spetz, and Joe Martin, and for some of the pictures from this side of 'the pond', my son Tim. The others were either taken by myself or come from Audi's own archives.

Ian Wagstaff

Introduction

Pedantically speaking, the Audi R8 was not a 'WSC Giant,' but for that we must blame motorsport's organising body, the Fédération Internationale de l'Automobile. In the early 1990s, the FIA, concerned, some said, that endurance racing could rival its hyped Formula 1 series, emasculated the then World Sports Car Championship with rules that decreed F1-sized engines and sprint races. By the end of 1992 the series had collapsed.

Since then the FIA has, perversely, decided that prototypes are no longer worthy of their own World Championship, bringing to an end a tradition that dated back to 1953[†]. When the FIA introduced a World Championship for sports cars – and even that was purely for GT cars – the Audi R8s were long gone. (It probably says something that, for a long time, the only FIA 'World' circuit racing championship other than Formula 1 was for Touring Cars – and a pair of 12 lappers for cars meant to look like mundane saloons was never going to challenge Grand Prix racing for preeminence.)

Thankfully, endurance sports car racing is one formula that can survive without a 'World' series, for it has the Le Mans 24 Hours, a race that transcends any championship. Despite something of a dip in the 1990s, Le Mans ensured that there were still manufacturers interested in showcasing their wares over a long distance race and, in 1999, Audi joined their ranks for the first time.

Le Mans and its organiser, the Automobile Club de l'Ouest, plus enthusiasts in North America, made sure that there were championships for the Audi R8 to contest, even if they did not have the 'World' title. In 1999, American businessman Don Panoz, with approval from the ACO, introduced the successful American Le Mans Series in which Audi rapidly became the leading player. Indeed, every year from 2000 to 2008, it was Audi that, in the top class (LMP, LMP900, and then LMP1), took the Chassis and Engine Manufacturers' Championships; it was Audi runners who took the Teams' Championship, and it was Audi pilots who won all the Drivers' Championships. A short-lived ALMS-backed European Le Mans Series took place in 2001 (won by an Audi driver), but was replaced in 2004 by the Le Mans Series (originally known as the Le Mans Endurance Series). It should come as no surprise that an Audi team and Audi drivers won that first year. In 2005 a sole R8 was fielded in the LMES, but despite some spirited performances by its drivers they could only manage joint fourth place in the drivers' title contest. It was the only seriously contested championship that the Audi R8 did not win. A 'WSC' Giant it may not have been, but a 'Giant' it certainly was.

One of the quickest drivers to have competed in an Audi R8, Allan McNish was in an Audi UK entry at Le Mans in 2004. (From an original painting by Ray Toombs)

[†]*As this book was going to press, the FIA and the ACO announced the creation of a FIA World Endurance Championship for 2012. After almost two decades, the prototypes were again being given the recognition they deserved.*

1999 – Audi R8C and R8R
New boys on the block

The Audi R8's podium lockout at the 2000 Le Mans 24 Hours had an inevitability about it that, arguably, belied the race's history. Le Mans is all about charismatic sports car names like Ferrari, Jaguar, Porsche, Aston Martin, Mercedes-Benz, or Bentley, but surely Audi was simply a worthy saloon car manufacturer? Indeed, prior to 1999 it had never competed at La Sarthe. Yet here its car had dominated the race in a way that had surprised few.

When four Audis arrived at the track the year before, they did so with purpose. But even those behind the programme can little have realised just how far the R8 and Le Mans would go to transform the very image of the company. True, Audi no longer had quite the staid image of a few years previously, thanks to its success in rallying and touring car racing and, in particular, to the iconic quattro, but it did not even have a sports car in its range. Yet, by the time the R8 had been replaced by the diesel-fuelled R10 in 2006, it had helped to turn Audi into one of the world's leading performance car manufacturers, as well as one of the all-time 'greats' of Le Mans. Audi even named a new GT car after it.

One could point to the fact that Audi had been part of the Auto Union amalgamation (along with DKW, Horch, and Wanderer) that had won Grands Prix in the 1930s, but while its Teutonic rival, Mercedes-Benz, had also contested long distance classics, and indeed won at Le Mans, Auto Union had not. (Audi's first competition success had come in the 1910 Swedish Reliability Trial.) Audi had also been at the forefront of rallying in the early 1980s, with the quattro winning two World Champion for Drivers titles and an equal number for Manufacturers. Success on the racetracks

Audi had been part of the Auto Union combine that competed in Grands Prix in the 1930s, winning first in the German Grand Prix of 1934, and finally at the 1939 Yugoslav Grand Prix. In the 1939 German Mountain Championship, held on the Grossglockner, H P Müller (pictured here) was fastest on the first leg of the climb, but lost out overall to Mercedes' Hermann Lang and the previous year's winner, team-mate Hans Stuck. (Courtesy Audi)

had also come the way of Audi touring cars. A TransAm championship was claimed in 1988, and then runners up position in the IMSA-GTO series the following year. Then came the 1990 German Touring Car Championship, the DTM, with the V8 quattro, and a couple more titles. From then on Audi concentrated on two-litre touring car racing, winning a number of national championships. In 1996 it took the national titles in seven different countries.

However, whatever way you looked at it, Audi was a new boy to sports car racing in 1999, having made the decision to enter this arena only two years before. (One might pedantically argue that the North American IMSA-GTO series was for GTs, but Audi's entry was based on the '90 quattro saloon.)

The 1999 season saw a high level of interest in Le Mans from the leading car manufacturers. Toyota, Mercedes-Benz, BMW, and Nissan all had prototypes in the lists, and there was even the last Ferrari to be entered in a prototype category at Le Mans. By the following year, all had gone; Toyota and BMW enticed by the siren Formula 1, which was ultimately to do no appreciable good for their images, and Mercedes-Benz understandably frightened by the spectre of the 1955 Le Mans disaster after its CLRs showed a tendency to take-off. In 2000, Audi's opposition was mainly a collection of specialist race car manufacturers plus an ill-fated effort from Cadillac, which had not been seen at Le Mans since 1950. That, though, shouldn't detract from Audi's progress, from third and fourth place the year before to overwhelming favourite for 2000. With Le Mans it is not so much the other cars that have to be beaten, but the race itself; Audi proved very early in its career at the track that it understood the best way to go about endurance racing. It built cars that could run fast and, so often, faultlessly for 24 hours and, as such, revolutionised expectations about the race. With the Audi R8, Le Mans became less a Grand Prix of endurance and more a 24 hour sprint race.

Roadster and coupé

In the beginning, or at least when they first raced, there were two cars; one a coupé developed in the UK, the other

It was arguably the quattro rally car, here leaping on the fearsome Epynt stages in Wales, that first put Audi on the competition map. (Author's collection)

Laurent Aiello (France)
One of two Audi Le Mans drivers to also come first in the Monaco GP Formula 3 support race, Laurent Aiello started twice at La Sarthe for the marque, before concentrating on the Deutsche Tourenwagen Masters (DTM). Aiello was a Le Mans winner, but not with Audi, having come first in 1998 driving a Porsche 911 GT1 with Allan McNish and Stéphane Ortelli, also both future R8 pilots. Aiello's greatest successes came in touring car racing, with first place in the 2002 DTM as well as the French Supertouring, German Super Touring, and British Touring Car championships in the 1990s. He was in Audi's winning team at Sebring in 2001.

The R8's predecessor, the R8R, set the stage with a podium place at Le Mans in 1999. (Courtesy Audi)

Hedging its bets, Audi management initially insisted that a coupé should also be run at Le Mans. (Courtesy Audi)

a roadster, fittingly, from Germany. Appropriately they were known as the R8C and R8R respectively. The newcomer to Le Mans was hedging its bets and it entered two of each kind for the 1999 24 hour race, perhaps unsure of the direction in which it should be heading. By the end of the contest it was apparent which way Audi had to go.

The black and silver open cars were entrusted into the hands of one of Le Mans' most experienced practitioners, Reinhold Joest, who had entered the winning Porsche engined cars in 1984 and 1985 (Porsche 956), and 1996

and 1997 (TWR-Porsche WSC95). There was, though, plenty that was Italian about the German roadsters, the monocoque having been designed by Dallara and built by ATR, whose operations were respectively based on the west and east coasts of that country. Fondmetal had assisted with the aerodynamics.

By contrast, the R8Cs were built by Volkswagen Group-owned RTN (Racing Technology Norfolk) in Higham, and run by Richard Lloyd's UK operation: Lloyd, like Joest, having been a notable Porsche entrant in endurance racing.

11

The closed cars shared the same rear drive train as the roadsters, including a new twin-turbo 3600cc V8 engine, the first purpose-made race engine from Audi since those of the Auto Unions. Both cars used longitudinal Ricardo gearboxes. (Noted Audi R8 engineer Brad Kettler was later to point out how rugged and serviceable these 'boxes were, saying: "Whoever designed them was a genius; they only won Le Mans five times. They were easy to work on and we did not need a load of special tools.") Otherwise, the two cars were very different, the heavier R8Cs competing in the LM GTP class, the R8Rs in the LMP category, which required that they used different sized air restrictors and Michelin tyres. In order to save weight, the R8Cs eschewed the power assisted steering used by the R8R.

Work first began on an Audi Le Mans car in August 1997, a time when indulgent rules were about to allow pseudo-GTs, such as the Porsche GT1-98, Toyota GT-One, and Nissan R390 GT1, to compete on a par with genuine prototypes. Audi felt the rules to be absurd, but thankfully this situation would not last long. By spring 1998 a 1:1 scale clay model was finished. Eight months into the work and wind tunnel testing began, initially with 1:4 and 1:2 models. In July, the first engine fired up on the test bed, and a month later a concept car was rolled out to run on Audi's own test track at Neustadt, near Ingolstadt. It was the first time that Audi had built a racing car with a carbon-fibre monocoque and mid-engine.

The first driver of that stark, black machine was Italian Rinaldo 'Dindo' Capello, who little can have realised what it would mean to his career. Frank Biela, Emanuele Pirro, and Yvan Müller also drove the car, although the latter was never to race it. In December, Audi boss Franz-Josef Paefgen presented the car to the international press in the Berlin Velodrom. Testing also took place at Most in the Czech Republic, and the Paul Ricard circuit in the south of France.

A man involved in the creation of both the R8R and R8C was Tony Southgate, the only designer to have won Le Mans, the Indianapolis 500, and Grands Prix, the former with the Group C Jaguars. Southgate, employed by Audi as a design consultant for 1999 and 2000, was first approached

by Dallara founder Gian Paolo Dallara to gauge his interest. The Englishman remembered: "They had built a prototype which was not very good and they needed some help." Southgate understood that whoever was responsible for the original, overweight design had now left. "It looked a bit like an Audi TT convertible with wings. It did not work, so it was an easy car to improve on. Audi should have started again but, if I had suggested that, I would have been out of a job."

Southgate recalled an extensive development programme. "By the time we got to Le Mans we were virtually on a mark three version. By then it was quite good and it looked completely different." The idea of a design consultant was, perhaps, foreign to some of the Audi Sport engineers. However, Southgate struck up a rapport with head of engine development Ulrich Baretzky, who he remembered was well supported by his chief designer Hartmut Diel. Project leader Wofgang Appel also impressed him, while he reckoned that resident aerodynamicist Michael Pfadenhauer, new to motor racing, was "... learning fast." It was evident that the Le Mans virgins were taking the 24 hour race very seriously indeed.

The Joest R8Rs, distinctive with their very low tails, raced first, finishing third and fifth at the Sebring 12 Hours driven by Michele Alboreto, Dindo Capello, and Stefan Johansson, and Perry McCarthy, Frank Biela, and Emanuele Pirro respectively. Although slow in qualifying for the Florida race – two seconds off the pace of the winning BMW – the ability to finish races, that was to

Tony Southgate, already a Le Mans-winning designer, was called in by Audi to assist with its sports car programme. (Courtesy Tony Southgate Collection)

be such a feature of the R8, appeared already there in its predecessor. By contrast, development of the R8Cs was somewhat rushed, one of them arriving for Le Mans prequalifying having completed only a few miles of testing at Snetterton, driven by the experienced Andy Wallace, and at Hockenheim.

Southgate, who had designed both closed and open cars for Le Mans in the past, had recommended to Audi that it concentrate just on the roadster. "I thought the regulations favoured this. You could run two inch wider tyres at the rear and that's a huge chunk of rubber." However, "the upper brass," as Southgate called them, were not convinced. They thought that the obviously more aerodynamic coupé was the way to go and, in September of the previous year, had asked him to design such a car. Theoretically, that meant the company would have an ideal comparison between the two types. It also saw Southgate "shuffling back and forth" between England and Germany. The R8C was one of the last cars that he was to draw himself. While he worked on the bodywork, Peter Elleray, who was to design the 2003 Le Mans-winning Bentley, concentrated on the chassis and suspension.

Time was short for the R8C design, which had to be passed by Christmas. Testing was carried out in the 'closed' Imperial College wind tunnel, unlike that of the R8R, which took place at SF's 'open' tunnel in Switzerland. Southgate was still 10 per cent down on the downforce numbers that he wanted, and with the narrower tyres that was a significant minus. Audi's own, new, full-scale tunnel at Ingolstadt was also used, but the work there on road cars meant time was limited.

The first R8C went to Snetterton for a shake down run, still all black and looking "very sinister." It was then painted and sent to Hockenheim, where Southgate recalled "it was OK but not as stable as it should have been under braking." At the Le Mans test day it was slightly quicker down the straights than the R8R, but not as much as it should have been. "I don't know why they have gone so late on the closed-top car," wrote rival Toyota driver Martin Brundle. "That's just silly."

In the meantime, Audi had been offered an automatic gearshift by Erwin Gassner's then small company, Megaline, that had been developed for motorcycle endurance racing. This, said Southgate, "was incredibly simple" and would enable the cars to be fitted with paddle shifts. The device was tested, and when the gearbox had been stripped down, the dog rings still appeared brand new. "That was when we realised that the pneumatic shift could give us a dramatic improvement in transmission reliability, which was just what you need for Le Mans." More gearshift conversions were ordered but only three could be made in time, so these were fitted to the two roadsters. The R8Cs raced, significantly as will be seen, with normal manual gearbox arrangements.

Andy Wallace, who raced both the R8C and, later for Champion Racing, the R8, pays tribute to the Megaline system which he was only able to experience with the latter. A veteran sports car racer by the time the Audi was first raced, he recalled how "terribly fragile" most race car gearboxes had been before the advent of the Audi. For him it was the control system that probably made all the difference. "Remember the R8C that I drove in 1999?" he was later to ask. "The R8Cs had similar gearboxes [to the R8R and R8] but they both blew up."

Le Mans

"We arrived as absolute nobodies in Le Mans," wrote head of Audi Motorsport, Dr Wolfgang Ullrich, after the race. However, in the days before he was reported to have said that Audi was aiming to beat race favourite Toyota "because if we did not believe that we could win the race, it would be better to stay at home."

Sebring R8R co-drivers Alboreto and Capello remained together for the 24 hour event and were joined by Laurent Aiello in chassis R8R-307. However, there had been a reshuffling of the drivers when Yvan Müller withdrew in mid-May for family reasons. Two drivers from the other Sebring car stayed together, Pirro and Biela sharing R8R-306 with Didier Theys. Johansson and McCarthy moved to the R8Cs, the Swede being joined in chassis 102 by Stéphane Ortelli and Christian Abt, the son of an Audi dealer; McCarthy by

The fourth place R8R, seen here rounding Mulsanne corner, was the subject of a rapid rear end change. (Author's collection)

Seiji Ara (Japan)

Fittingly, it was Seiji Ara who was at the wheel of the Japanese-entered Team Goh R8 as it completed its final, winning laps at Le Mans in 2004. A regular in the Japanese Super GT Championship, Ara won three times in his ten appearances with the Goh R8, but perhaps was not the star driver that Japan craved. In 2010 he signed with Swiss Racing Team to contest the FIA GT Championship in a Nissan GT-R. Since his Audi days, Ara has competed at Le Mans for Team Goh in a Porsche Spyder and also twice raced there in a Dome.

fellow Brits James Weaver and Andy Wallace in 101. With the exception of Weaver, all would go on to race the R8 itself at some time in the coming years.

With less drag and larger restrictors, the 15cm longer R8Cs were quicker in terms of outright speed. However, it was probably poorer road holding and hasty preparation that meant they were slower than the R8Rs at the end of the pit straight, thanks to their exit speed from the Ford chicane. In practice, the roadsters lapped quicker than the coupés, Capello, fastest of all four, being 8.2 seconds ahead of Wallace. The Joest team had also shown how fast it could change the rear end of the R8R. A time of 4 mins 56 secs in practice indicated that it might be possible to repeat the exercise in the race without losing track position.

Ullrich had actually been saying, since right back to the launch of its Le Mans programme in December

Audi employed the resources of serial Le Mans winner Reinhold Joest (left), seen here with his technical director, Ralf Jüttner. (Courtesy Audi)

1998, that Audi was intending to win Le Mans first time out. In the event, its cars were obviously slower than the victorious BMW, the Toyotas, and the Mercedes-Benz, but the eventual third and fourth places for the roadsters impressed most people. "We were like a beginner," recalled Capello, who was in the fourth finishing car.

Both the less service friendly coupés suffered from gear selection troubles throughout qualifying, problems which reoccurred within the first couple of hours of the race; a

"We arrived as absolute nobodies," wrote Dr Wolfgang Ullrich. (Courtesy Audi)

factor that would have an effect on the design of the R8 to come. Indeed, the Wallace/Weaver/McCarthy car was the first to pit for major repairs, 45 minutes being lost to a gearbox change. The other car seemed to be overcoming its early race problems. However, with Abt at the wheel, it stopped at the entry to Les Hunaudieres just before 8.00pm. The Audi UK mechanics went out to the car to discover a broken differential. The roadsters were doing better, and by this stage in the race the Theys/Pirro/Biela R8R was up to fifth place.

At 8.20 the next morning McCarthy brought his car to a halt just before the Hunaudieres hump. It too had been experiencing gearbox maladies, which had put it back to last in the prototype category during the night. Just after midnight it had been forced to spend 75 minutes in its garage. By 2.00pm the leading R8R was temporarily up to third place. It then settled back into fourth for many hours, until the leading BMW had an accident at 11.55am.

The second of the roadsters also experienced a gearbox problem, as well as having to have its exhausts changed, but finished the race, a rear end replacement taking place exactly has had been demonstrated in practice. It looked almost like a routine stop. Audi was obviously on a learning curve, but as Ullrich was to point

Audi UK retains one of the R8Cs, occasionally bringing it out for promotional purposes. (Author's collection)

Frank Biela (Germany)

Frank Biela was the 'winningest' driver in an R8, with 21 victories from 55 starts. These included three Le Mans victories and two ALMS titles. It was also he who, in avoiding a slower car, missed the pit lane entry and ran out of fuel at Le Mans in 2003. A member of the trio that took three consecutive wins from 2000 to 2002, Neuss-born Biela returned to the top step of the rostrum at Le Mans in 2007 and 2008 with the R10. Having also won the DTM and the French and British Touring Car Championships for the marque, he is thought to have taken more championship titles for Audi than any other driver. For him, though, the R8 was "definitely the most important car in my career."

out later, it was about to painstakingly implement the lessons that it had just leaned. It should be pointed out that, even this early in Audi's Le Mans career, the pit stops went well.

"I thought third and fourth was a good result for first time but Audi did not agree," said Southgate. "I was told by one of the directors that third was the minimum it could accept. They were green then and thought they could win first time out." That 'greenness' would not last long.

Audi R8C 1999 specifications

Vehicle type: Le Mans GT Prototype (LM-GTP)
Monocoque: Carbon fibre (development partner rtn), crash structure FIA and ACO approved, steel safety cage
Body: Carbon fibre
Engine: V8, turbocharged, 90-degree cylinder angle, 4 valves per cylinder, 2 Garrett turbochargers; to comply with the rules 2x33.9mm air restrictors, and boost pressure restriction to 1.87bar (absolute)
Engine management: Bosch MS 2.8
Engine lubrication: Dry sump, Shell Racing Oil SR
Displacement: 3600cc
Output: 640bhp @ 6300rpm
Torque: 760Nm @ 5750rpm
Power transmission: Rear-wheel drive
Clutch: CFRP clutch
Gearbox: Sequential 6-speed sports gearbox, partner Ricardo
Differential: Multiple-disc limited-slip differential
Steering: Mechanical rack-and-pinion steering, not servo-assisted
Suspension: Independent double-wishbone suspension front and rear. Pushrod system with horizontal spring/damper unit, adjustable gas-filled shock absorbers
Brakes: Hydraulic dual-circuit brake system, monobloc light-alloy brake callipers, ventilated carbon fibre discs front and rear, brake force distribution, driver adjustable
Rims: OZ forged magnesium rims, Front: 12.25x18in, Rear: 13x18in
Tyres: Michelin Radial, Front: 29/65-18, Rear: 31/71-18
Length: 4800cm
Width: 2000cm
Height: 980cm
Minimum weight: 900kg
Tank capacity: 90 litres

Audi R8R 1999 specifications

Vehicle type: Le Mans Prototype (LMP)
Monocoque: Carbon fibre, crash structure FIA and ACO approved, steel safety bars front and rear
Body: Carbon fibre
Engine: V8, turbocharged, 90-degree cylinder angle, 4 valves per cylinder, 2 Garrett turbochargers; to comply with the rules 2x33.2mm air restrictors, and boost pressure restriction to 1.67bar (absolute)
Engine management: Bosch MS 2.8
Engine lubrication: Dry sump, Shell Racing Oil SR
Displacement: 3600cc
Output: 610bhp @ 6300rpm
Torque: 700Nm @ 5750rpm
Power transmission: Rear-wheel drive
Clutch: CFRP clutch
Gearbox: Sequential 6-speed sports gearbox, partner Ricardo
Differential: Multiple-disc limited-slip differential
Steering: Servo-assisted rack-and-pinion steering
Suspension: Independent double-wishbone suspension front and rear. Pushrod system with horizontal spring/damper unit, adjustable gas-filled shock absorbers
Brakes: Hydraulic dual-circuit brake system, monobloc light-alloy brake callipers, ventilated carbon fibre discs front and rear, brake force distribution, driver adjustable
Rims: OZ forged magnesium rims, Front: 13x18in, Rear: 14.5x18in
Tyres: Michelin Radial, Front: 32/65-18, Rear: 36/71-18
Length: 4650cm
Width: 1080cm
Height: 1080cm
Minimum weight: 900kg
Tank capacity: 90 litres

2000 – Audi R8R and R8
The pattern is set

Apart from Ulrich Baretsky's V8 engine, there was nothing the same about the thoroughly detailed R8 that first turned a wheel at Neustadt on December 23, 1999. Audi Sport director Dr Wolfgang Ullrich totally revised the project and abandoned any idea of a coupé. The result, designed by a team led by Wolfgang Appel, Audi Sport's head of vehicle technology, with Michael Pfadenhauer looking after the aerodynamics and described by Ullrich as "revolutionary," was about to show the sports car world what Teutonic efficiency really meant. (While the engineering and design was carried out by Audi, the chassis of the R8, like the R8R, was actually produced by the Italian specialist racing car manufacturer Dallara.)

The R8R was wheeled out at Charlotte, where Biela and Pirro finished sixth. A spin dropped the Capello/Alboreto/ McNish car out of contention. The use of combined oval and road courses proved unpopular, and the ALMS quickly dropped them from its schedule. (Courtesy Audi)

In class terms, the Audi R8R had competed in the LMP category, and the R8C in the LM GTP grouping. For 2000, changes had been made, and the R8 was classified as an LMP 900, such cars weighing no less than 900kg and having a maximum of either 6.0-litre normally-aspirated or 4.0-litre turbocharged engines. (A second, lighter and less powerful class, LMP 675, was also introduced that year.)

Rinaldo 'Dindo' Capello (Italy)

Grey-haired, dependable Dindo Capello must have wondered what it took to win Le Mans in an R8. He followed up third place in 2000 with a pair of seconds and then won the race, but in a Bentley. However, he put his Le Mans R8 jinx behind him when he was one of the drivers of the winning Team Goh car in 2004. A third Le Mans victory followed in 2008 with the diesel Audi R10. Audi dealer Capello's loyalty to the marque must be the longest, as he drove first an Audi 80 and then an A4 quattro in the Italian Super Touring Car Championship from 1994 to 1998, winning the series in 1996, and was also one of those who competed in the R8R. The R8 gave him 19 victories from 40 races.

Tony Southgate, who was still involved, although less so than in 1999, recalled: "The Audi engineers were now in their stride. By the time they had got to the R8 they had learnt a lot. It was massively better and, unlike the R8R, looked as if it had been designed as one." Appel wrote that the aim had been to simultaneously achieve two goals; to go faster, and yet become more "maintenance friendly."

The question of an open or closed car had been answered by Audi, at least for the next decade, although, as Wolfgang Appel was to recall, "... many people told me

the coupé was a nicer car." While Audi may have decided to go with the roadster concept in 2000, this is a subject that has remained unresolved in endurance racing to this day. When Peugeot entered the fray in 2007, it did so with a coupé specifically because that was the only way it felt it could compete with its German rival. "We had to make something different. Nobody can do a better open car than Audi," said Peugeot technical director Bruno Famin.

Audi was to remain in the roadster camp with the R8's immediate successors, the diesel R10 and R15. It was only in 2011, with the R18, that Audi built a coupé again, just as Aston Martin went in the opposite direction, from a closed to an open prototype. In 2007, a year after the R8's last appearance, Appel's preference for a roadster was obvious. "You have problems with the structure of coupés, with the doors, with the cooling, so most designers prefer an open car." Pointing to the rain during practice for Sebring that year, he stated how, unlike street-going production roadsters, open race cars are more suited to such conditions than closed ones.

By 2011, new rules specifying less powerful engines saw the emphasis change to maximum aerodynamic efficiency, while the reduction from four to two mechanics changing tyres meant there was less emphasis on a quick driver change, something that was easier with an open car. Thus, Audi reverted to a coupé for the first time since the R8C. There were those who pointed to a similarity between the shape of the R18, created by its chief aerodynamicist Martin Gershbacher, and the Bentley Speed 8, which itself had implemented lessons learned from that earlier car. Twelve years on, an R8 legacy was still apparent. Indeed, Audi stated that it had drawn on the experiences gained in 1999 although, unlike the R8C, the carbon fibre monocoque of the R18 did not consist of two halves, but featured a single-component design to save weight and increase stiffness. If nothing else, when asked at the launch of the R18 what Audi had learned from the R8C that had helped with the new car, Dr Ullrich, who regretted the necessity of going closed, quickly retorted: "We learned the importance of fitting strong door latches!"

It was now an easy matter to change the whole rear end of the car. (Courtesy Gary Horrocks)

Audi had not competed on an international stage quite like the one it stood on in 2000 since the Auto Union Grand Prix days. Preparation was again entrusted to Reinhold Joest. Joest's 60-strong staff joined the 130 people working on the R8 at Audi. One feels that the legendary Alfred Neubauer, although he had been team manager of Auto Union's rival Mercedes-Benz, would have approved of the way Audi was now going racing.

One attention to detail that had been learnt from the previous year's gearbox problems, was the fact that on the new R8, the suspension and the rear wing were mounted on the gearbox casing, which was behind the differential. This meant that, if the Ricardo 'box or a rear drive train component had to be changed, the whole unit including the gearbox, suspension, brakes, and wheels could be quickly replaced by a new one. Damaged rear suspension on two of the cars meant that this did happen at Le Mans, the whole job taking a matter of just seven minutes. One

former winner, the authoritative Paul Frère, suggested that this might be against the spirit of endurance racing.

It should be pointed out that, at this stage, the coupé programme was not dead. Peter Elleray and Tony Southgate, who was to leave Audi just 12 days after the R8's first Le Mans victory, continued to work on this after the 1999 race. Improvements were made in the wind tunnel and it became the basis for the Bentley EXP Speed 8 that appeared in 2001. The successor to this was to win at Le Mans two years later, breaking up the R8's run of victories there.

Having been unveiled to the public in Miami in March, the Michelin-shod Audi R8s started their racing life as they meant to continue. Their debut race, the 2000 Sebring 12 Hours, saw a pair that battled for lead for the duration. The American Le Mans Series, of which the Florida race was a round, was now considered to be the world's major sports car championship and it was fitting that Audi's first ever major sports car win should come at such a prestigious event.

"The R8 first showed me the strengths of the Audi Sport team," said Dindo Capello, seen here at the car's debut in Sebring. (Courtesy Martin Spetz)

The Joest-run R8s had been the class of the field throughout practice and qualifying, and they had taken the airfield circuit's notorious bumps in their stride. However, it has to be recorded that one Tom Kristensen, making his debut in the car, locked up a front wheel under braking and went off the track early in the first qualifying session, right under the nose of Dr Ullrich. The following day, Frank Biela claimed the R8's first pole with the now repaired car.

From the start the R8s outdistanced the rest of the field, with the Frank Biela/Tom Kristensen/Emanuele Pirro car, distinguished by the colour red, the quicker of the pair. Initially they were chased by a couple of Panoz, one of which took the lead when the front-running Audi was delayed by ignition troubles. The Panoz fell out of the reckoning, leaving one of the BMWs to take up the fight. Pit strategy enabled this to remain within striking distance until the last hour. However, the end was all about the Audis. Allan McNish had moved to the front in the eighth hour, in the second R8, after a long stop for its rival to bleed the brakes. The Scot and Dindo Capello were now carrying out all the driving duties in this car, their team-mate, five-time Grand Prix-winner Michele Alboreto not having been comfortable in the car all weekend.

Despite brake problems, and just one headlight to cope with the encroaching dark, McNish was putting on a performance that would become typical of his drives for Audi in the coming years. Pirro, though, caught up to within 54 seconds following a yellow flag period. Rather than pit under this, McNish had not been called in until the green flag was waved again. Capello now took over the brakeless car and, with a spin half an hour before the end, was unable to hold off his fellow Italian, coming home 30 seconds behind.

"The R8 first showed me the strengths of the Audi Sport team," recalled Capello. "In a few months they had built us a car that was far better than the R8R. I had no experience of sports cars before the R8R but there was no comparison between the two cars; they were like night and day. It was something unbelievable, probably the biggest step forward that a manufacturer has done in motorsport."

Kristensen had been in the opposition camp the year before. "When I was with BMW I had been able to drive circles around the R8R. The main problem with the R8R was the rear geometry, but when I drove the interim car in 2000 the problem had already been solved. When the full spec R8 was introduced many people said that they had never seen a car that could run so soft but still be efficient aerodynamically. The ride was fantastic in 2000 but, over the years, we got even better. We were able to race it on slow tracks, fast tracks, bumpy tracks, and flat tracks. With changes in setup we were able to get the car to work on many kinds of surface.

"The BMW was the state of the art in 1999, but the engine was not so much of a monkey on your shoulder as a gorilla. The Audi was the first sports car that I drove that did not have any big disadvantages. Admittedly, there were things, the first year was probably understeer and a very aggressive engine with the turbo, but these were things that were worked on over the years."

Southgate remembered how relieved Baretzky and his team had appeared when, at a meeting, he pointed out he would rather have an engine based on reliability than power for Le Mans. "That was a revelation for the Audi men." According to Southgate, the three Audis at Le Mans that year were producing less than 600 horsepower. "Our best engine was 597bhp. Nobody believed us. They were all convinced we had about 650hp." Audi was later to claim 610bhp for the original engines. However, rule restrictions introduced during the subsequent life of the R8 reduced the figure to around 520bhp by the time it was retired in 2006.

McNish, a Le Mans winner with Porsche in 1997, recalled how he found himself in an R8. "I looked around. Toyota was out [he had driven for the Japanese concern in 1999], Porsche was out. I had seen how Audi had under performed in 1999, but it had still finished on the podium. Its history in motorsport seemed to be that it dipped its toe into the water and then went gung ho.

"In its initial form, I did not like driving the R8; I preferred the R8R. It took until Le Mans for me to get comfortable and confident with the car. It was very fast but the throttle response was aggressive and it was brutal. Aerodynamically it was good, but it was quite pitchy to drive. By the time we got to Le Mans Audi was starting to sort out the aero and the engine.

"The 1999 R8R was old-fashioned but we had no comparison with the past," said engine man Baretzky. "However, in 2000 we made a big, big step and the car is a legend now."

While it was wondered at the time if Audi would be able to enjoy the advantage that it undoubtedly had at Sebring, elsewhere, the German marque had, almost overnight, established itself as a major force in endurance racing. The ultimate test of this discipline, the Le Mans 24 Hours was just three months away, this being the next race on Audi's calendar after the Sebring shakedown. Already, despite having only competed once at Sarthe, it seemed a firm favourite for victory.

Ullrich, who admitted to having been fascinated by Le Mans even as a youngster, pointed to the fact that the team had experienced a few problems with pit stops – it was not quite yet the epitome of efficiency that it was to become – but the R8 had been the fastest car at Sebring. The only technical problem had been those fading brakes. "We will get them sorted," said team boss Reinhold Joest.

Between Sebring and Le Mans, Audi kept its hand in by entering a couple of R8Rs for the second and third rounds of the ALMS. A sixth for Biela and Pirro was the best place at Charlotte, the Capello/Alboreto/McNish car dropping out of contention following a spin. At Silverstone the two cars finished third and fourth, with Capello and McNish on the podium.

Le Mans

The finish of the 2000 Le Mans 24 Hours set the scene for most of the next five years. Three Audi R8s, their national silver livery bespattered with the detritus of 24 hours of racing, crossed the line in perfect formation, the second and third cars fractionally behind, with Emanuele Pirro in the lead car, both arms high in the air, waving an Audi flag. Each was distinguished by a colour from the German flag; red, yellow, or black. It was a sight that probably crushed the heart out of the opposition until the advent of the diesel era.

A foregone conclusion was how some described the result, following Audi's performance at the April test day and during official practice. The massed factory ranks of the previous year had already melted away. The Cadillacs and Chryslers that had taken over from the manufacturers who had made the 1999 race so fascinating, were inexperienced and only Panoz seemed to have any chance of beating the German cars, which weighed 902kg; a figure very close to the 900kg minimum.

During qualifying something happened which, in the

The R8s await their inaugural Le Mans. (Author's collection)

25

Aiello was to race an R8 just once more, but McNish and Ortelli would be reunited in an Audi during 2005. (Author's collection)

light of the R8's subsequent history, was unusual to say the least. Christian Abt came to a halt at the end of the pit road with a broken piston. It was never discovered why, and the R8 engines went on to record a remarkable record of reliability; several of them clocked in excess of 10,000 kilometres.

From the moment honorary starter Jacky Ickx dropped the flag, it seemed that even those manufacturers who remained had already given up, although David Brabham's Panoz did give chase. The Australian was the only person ever to lead the Joest run cars, and that was when Panoz team manager David Price used a yellow flag period and an early pit stop to produce a false picture that only lasted four laps. Otherwise, pole sitter Allan McNish led the opening laps, was the first one to overtake Brabham, and led until team-mate Michele Alboreto went ahead, when, during the third round of stops, he only took on fuel. The number eight car, distinguished by its red highlights and driven by Frank Biela, Tom Kristensen, and Pirro, looked the least likely of the trio, and it was not until well into the third hour that slick pit work saw it come out ahead of the dogged Panoz.

The McNish/Aiello/Ortelli R8 was an early leader in 2000, the first time that an Audi had led at the Le Mans 24 Hours. (Author's collection)

The Kristensen/Biela/Pirro R8 rounding the Ford chicane on its way to Audi's first, seemingly inevitable, Le Mans victory. (Author's collection)

Ten hours into the race, the Panoz that Brabham shared with Jan Magnussen and Mario Andretti was already two laps down on the Audis; when that pitted to have the gearbox pinions replaced, that was pretty much it. The three R8s did battle amongst themselves, but crucially for the number eight, it was the only one that did not have to undergo a gearchange during the night (these were performed in just over six minutes). From the eleventh hour it controlled the proceedings, despite pressure from the yellow distinguished number nine of McNish, Laurent Aiello, and Stéphane Ortelli. A brake disc change by the leader allowed McNish back onto the lead lap in the morning. In the final minutes he dutifully allowed himself to be lapped, so that the photographers could record just how crushing the Audi victory had been. It is, perhaps, too easy to point to the lack of credible opposition. What should be remembered

The start of yet another lap. The Audi R8s were inexorable on their way to a triumphant one, two, three. (Author's collection)

Contemplating the long day ahead.
(Courtesy Tim Wagstaff)

is that maximum boost pressure for turbocharged engines had been lowered from the previous year, and air restriction increased. Yet, the winning Audi still travelled 40 kilometres further than 1999's victorious BMW.

Kristensen scored the second of his many Le Mans victories accompanied by Biela and Pirro, the first of what was to be an amazing hat-trick of 24 Hours wins for the trio. A lap behind were Aiello, Ortelli, and an on-fire McNish, who had set the pole as well as establishing fastest lap on the car's 233rd circuit. These three had won for Porsche in 1998 and were seen as an attempt to win the race with the same drivers, but a different manufacturer. In third place came Alboreto, Christian Abt, and Dindo Capello, who was, some years hence, to join the list of Audi R8 Le Mans winners.

Around the world

A month after the Le Mans triumph, the American Le Mans Series was again away from its native land, this time at the Nürburgring, and Audi, despite being on its home soil, fell from the heights with a proverbial bump on a cold and wet day. In practice, the two R8s looked as if they were continuing where they had left off but, right from the green light, things went wrong. Jan Magnussen, in his Panoz, immediately shot past them, while a pair of BMWs also took them on as they struggled to get any heat into their Michelin tyres. Matters only got worst, with a premature pit stop, wrong tyre choices, engine cut out, and spins for McNish – the second of which resulted in the floor being ripped from the car. The other R8 of Biela and Pirro came home third, three laps down. At this point one might have thought that Audi was not as impregnable as the Sebring and Le Mans results had indicated. One would have been wrong. It was to be the R8's only defeat of the year. Indeed, it would 12 months before it was beaten to the chequered flag again.

The ALMS returned to North America and a sequence of eight Audi victories to finish off the season. The rain of the Eifel mountains gave way to the sunshine of California, as the R8s showed what they were really capable of and lapped the entire field at Sears Point. It was the first victory in an R8 for Capello and McNish, the latter on superlative form. It was also the first win for chassis R8-403, which had been seen at all three races so far. From now on, it and R8-405, which had made its debut at the Nürburgring, would constitute Audi's attack on the 2000 series.

The pair continued their winning ways at Mosport but with Capello electing to finish the race on wet tyres, despite a rapidly drying track and Jörg Müller having slicks on his BMW; it was no easy victory. BMW caught Audi on the final lap, but could just not get past, the 0.148 second margin of victory being the closest in ALMS history. Pirro, who was on slicks in the other R8, with 11 minutes to go, collided with a GT and was forced into retirement.

It was Pirro and Biela's turn to win at Texas Motor Speedway in R8-405, but only because of a faulty pits-to-car radio in its sister R8. McNish and Capello controlled an arduously hot race from the beginning, but the Italian was unable to hear when the team called him in for a final fuel stop under yellow flags. He continued to the end of his fuel allocation but, by now, the track was green and Biela was able to convert a 17 second deficit into a similarly sized lead, holding on for a further nine laps until the flag.

Although there were still five races to go on the 2000 ALMS calendar, it was already known that McNish would have to put his sports car career on hold, having signed up for a testing role with the Toyota Formula 1 outfit. Ullrich was on record that he would like to retain the Scot's services, a wise observation as it turned out. There was also conjecture that, while Audi was expected to return to the ALMS the following season, it might not be with the Joest team. The series organisers wanted to see R8s in private hands.

Meanwhile, the ALMS year continued on with roles reversed for the Audi pair at Portland. This time McNish and Capello fell right back after colliding with a GT in the early stages, only for the Biela/Pirro car to encounter the safety car immediately after its first fuel stop, causing it to lose a lap to the chasing pack. Capello and McNish caught up and went on to win the 2 hour 45 min race by almost a lap.

Some ALMS races are more prestigious than others, and in its relatively short history the Petit Le Mans 10 Hour contest at Road Atlanta has become one of endurance racing's most important. McNish was again the dominant force, but the Panoz and BMWs were back to being dangerous. Numerous yellow flags helped to keep them in touch but, in the end, most of them hit trouble and Capello strolled home in the car that he shared with the Scot and Alboreto. McNish was now in the lead of the championship. In second place was the other R8, Kristensen back to share the driving with Biela and Pirro. Halfway through the race, this car's rear diffuser was torn off in a collision, and on the run to the chequered flag and second place it was less than a second ahead of Jan Magnussen's Panoz. The Dane complained that, as he chased down the R8 in those final laps, he had been held up by the sister Audi of Capello, a healthy three laps ahead and splitting the two warring cars on the track.

On, then, to Laguna Seca; a turbulent race and another one-two. However, a botched start meant that the R8 pair were initially down in fourth and fifth and did not establish themselves at the head of the field until the second half of the race, when the leading Panoz's engine failed. Again, it was McNish and Capello who came home first, despite three collisions – one of which caused the Scot to utter serious words about BMW driver Jean-Marc Gounon – and a spin. The ALMS manufacturers' title was now wrapped up, and McNish was setting his sights on the drivers' championship.

Las Vegas was one of those unsatisfactory tracks where an infield 'road course' joined up half of a conventional banked oval. Biela and Pirro were back on the top step of the podium for the first time since Texas, the pair having benefited when the three cars ahead of them – Muller's BMW, Capello's Audi, and David Brabham's Panoz – were involved in a spectacular melee. The consensus of opinion was that this was one race Panoz did deserve to win, but in the end it was an Audi one-two again. To all intents and purposes, McNish had the title.

The ALMS again left America for the final race of the series, in fact the final day of the year 2000, which gave it a 'Race of Two Thousand Years' tag. The venue was the streets of Adelaide, and Audi celebrated this in appropriate fashion by giving R8-403 a garish crocodile livery. One of the largest crowds in the series' history turned up to watch what was its first street race. Capello had a spectacular accident in warm up, while McNish was suffering from a back strain – said to have been caused when removing his kilt – but still the season's most successful pairing took the win, and in McNish's case, secured the ALMS drivers' title. Statistically only Capello could have overtaken him, and he was in the same car. (Australian Touring Car Champion Brad Jones, who had difficulty fitting into the cockpit, had been standing by in case McNish's back was too bad.) Pirro, in the second R8, brushed the wall when lapping a slower car, causing a delay of over an hour. As a result, he and Biela could only manage 16th place at the finish.

McNish was now on his way to Formula 1 with Toyota, and would not be seen in an R8 again until 2004. When he returned, changes to the engine configuration would have made the car a different animal.

Laguna Seca was a turbulent race, but resulted in another Audi one-two. (Courtesy Gary Horrocks)

The somewhat garish crocodile livery used at Adelaide in 2000 was brought out nine years later for the Goodwood Festival of Speed. (Courtesy Audi)

2001 – Audi R8
An engine change

The year 2001 would be a busy one for the now well-established Audi R8s. Joest was still going to run a couple of cars in the ALMS, as well as the new affiliated European Le Mans Series. However, two Audi R8s had now escaped from factory hands. Chassis R8-403, with which the McNish/Capello pairing had enjoyed so much success, had been sold to English collector and amateur driver Phil Bennett, to be raced by a team run by Mike Earle's Arena Motorsport for former Grand Prix driver Stefan Johansson. Likewise, R8-405 had been bought by the American team Champion Racing, a fact that was announced at a gala press launch in Pompano Beach, Florida. Team director Dave Maraj, who could see the way things were going and had sold his Lola, reckoned that the R8 elevated his team from amateur to professional status. Maraj had founded Champion Racing back in 1994, as one of the entities of the Champion Group that included Audi and Porsche dealerships.

Unusually, the season did not begin on the featureless wastes of Sebring, though it did start with yet another Audi one-two. Not only had these now become commonplace, but, over the next two races, such a result would become eclipsed as Audis took the first four places at Sebring, and then the first three at Donington Park. But first to Audi's second appearance, at the Texas Motor Speedway. Such was the pace of Panoz's new LMP07, not to mention one of its older cars, that there were predictions that Audi might not have it all its own way this year. It was, though, a false dawn, and Capello, with new partner Kristensen, won ahead of the familiar Biela/Pirro duo. For the first time at an ALMS race, three Audi R8s were entered. The Champion car had a certain amount of bad luck and finished fourth

behind one of the Panoz. However, it was pointed out that neither of its drivers – 1988 Le Mans winner Andy Wallace, and American Dorsey Schroeder – had tested the car prior to the event. Champion's position at the top of the podium would have to wait until 2003.

It was a new chassis R8-502 that started off the season in fine fashion, following up the Texas win with victories at Sebring and Donington. Of its Texas drivers, only Capello was still at the wheel for Sebring, being joined by Alboreto and Laurent Aiello. Biela, Kristensen, and Pirro had another chassis that had made its debut at Dallas, R8-503. Ralph Kelleners joined Wallace and Schroeder for Champion. For the first time a fourth R8 lined up on the grid. This was the Johansson car, driven by the Swede himself and Guy Smith, who was to go on to win Le Mans for Bentley in 2003. What made the latter car striking was its powder blue and orange livery, its Gulf sponsorship meaning that it enjoyed the iconic colours made famous by the John Wyer Porsche 917s – particularly in Steve McQueen's film, 'Le Mans.'

As the previous year, the Audis dominated Sebring, the difference between the two Joest cars being the time spent in the pits, an electronic fault having delayed R8-503, while R8-502 merely had to have its front brake pads changed. A stop-go penalty, incurred when Kristensen exceeded the pit lane speed limit by a full 10kmh, put paid to a late attempt by the Dane to catch up the Aiello/Alboreto/Capello car. A sad observation is that this was the last ever victory for former Ferrari Grand Prix driver Alboreto. A month after his win, the approachable Italian was killed testing an R8 at the EuroSpeedway, Lausitzring in Germany. He had raced R8s on four occasions, winning on two, as well as having driven

The famed Gulf orange and powder blue livery reappeared on Stefan Johansson's privately entered car at Sebring in 2001. (Courtesy Martin Spetz)

Johnny Herbert (England)

Johnny Herbert was seen as one of the most promising drivers of his generation until a serious Formula 3000 accident left him with severe injuries. Nevertheless, he made a remarkable comeback to make it into Formula 1. Twice he won Grands Prix for Benetton, and once for Stewart. He then became one of the few men to have won both World Championship races and at Le Mans, when he came first at La Sarthe in 1991 for Mazda. He took fastest lap for Bentley there in 2003, and then pole position the following year with a Team Veloqx R8. Herbert drove R8s from 2001 to 2003 for Champion, competed at Sebring and Le Mans in 2002 for the factory team, and contested the 2004 LMES with the UK squad, winning the championship that year with Jamie Davies. During this time he totalled eight wins with the car.

an R8R in 1999. He had previously driven long distance sports cars for the Lancia factory in the 1980s, and won at Le Mans in 1997 with Joest. Wolfgang Ullrich described the accident, thought to have been caused by tyre failure, as an "incomprehensible tragedy." The Audi R8 was one of the safest, most robust cars built, but motor racing can never be totally safe; all the cars were subsequently fitted with an energy diffuser mounted on the rear of the monocoque. Joest transporters now carry a sticker with Alboreto's name and the words 'Danke Dir' ('Thanks for All').

Four laps behind the works cars at Sebring came the Champion entry, the Gulf car being a further four laps back following electrical problems. Johansson, who had stayed long in the car, reckoned that the battery cables had been laid wrongly when the car was built. The new Panoz LMP07

retired with gearbox problems, having never troubled the Audis, and the eventual fifth place car, a Lola-Judd, was way back – some 38 laps behind. When it came to the truly long races, Audi really did show its competence.

But now for something different. In an attempt to ape the success of its North American series, the organisers of the ALMS initiated a European Le Mans Series, the first two rounds of which, Donington and Jarama, had been joined with the ALMS ensuring three Audi R8s on the grid. The other races, on the Estoril and Most circuits, did not count for ALMS points, which would account for the fact that, of the R8 runners, only Johansson attended.

At Donington, famed for its pre-war Grands Prix, two of which were won by Auto Union, Capello and Kristensen recorded an excellent win despite another stop-go

The change to TFSI engines was achieved in secrecy, the first that the public knew of this being after the victory at Le Mans. (Author's collection)

penalty, while Biela and Pirro lost a lap due to a puncture. Nevertheless, the three R8s finished first, second, and third, four and five laps ahead of the next contender. It was said that there were now three classes of prototype in endurance racing; LM675, LMP900, and Audi R8. Johansson, observing the Joest team, reckoned it to be probably the best that there had ever been in sports car racing. Any hope for its rivals must have fallen when Wolfgang Ullrich said at Donington that Audi would probably continue in sports car racing the following year, despite the fact that this would mean it would again be going head-to-head at Le Mans for a second year with its sister marque within the Volkswagen Group, Bentley.

Capello and Kristensen again won in Spain, where their car was R8-501, the first of the second generation R8s. Perhaps more significant, was the fact that this was the first race in that an R8 was fitted with a TFSI engine. Producing more power and more torque, and using less fuel, this power plant had been developed in such secrecy that few were aware that it was being used in Spain. Indeed, the first that the public knew about it was after the victory at Le Mans the following month. It was the development of the TFSI, the only engine to use a combination of direct fuel injection and turbochargers, and the subsequent use of this technology in road cars, that Ulrich Baretzky believes best justifies Audi's involvement in motorsport.

Ulrich Baretzky points out how the Le Mans TFSI programme has benefited Audi's road-going range. (Author's collection)

The heavens opened at Le Mans in 2001. (Courtesy Audi)

"We achieved an awful lot by developing this engine. People ask me how I can sleep at night when my engines are producing so much CO_2. However, since 2006, three million cars have been produced by the Volkswagen Group using FSI, and if each of those does just 10,000 kilometres with a reduction of fuel consumption of 10 per cent, that means a saving of three billion litres of fuel. It's a lake! By introducing this technology we forced BMW, Mercedes-Benz, and others to follow, so it is an even bigger saving."

Between the start of the TSFI programme and Le Mans there was to be just 15 months. An engine ran on the dyno, initially, in November 2000, and for the first time in a car the following February. Baretzky recalled that there were plenty of problems that had to be solved, particularly with the high-pressure pumps, the final version being received from Bosch just ten days before the race. Although the R8 last raced in

2006, development of the FSI continued for road cars in such a way that both power and economy continued to improve.

At Jarama the factory cars had been engaged in an enthralling duel with the Johansson R8, until the Swede left the road after a pebble had chaffed its way through a brake line. Although the car was to win at Most, that was in the absence of works competition. In Spain, Johansson had actually been leading when he began to feel his brake pedal lengthen; fourth place for him and Guy Smith, following repairs, was scant reward. Second was the other Joest R8, it having been Pirro on this occasion who had had his wrists slapped with a stop-go penalty, in this case for overtaking a lapped car under the yellow flags. For all four R8s, racing Le Mans now loomed ... only it was not the only thing that loomed. Some threatening rain clouds did, too.

Dindo Capello is probably relieved to be in the pits. Conditions at Le Mans in 2001 were the worst for years. (Courtesy Audi)

Le Mans

The Volkswagen Group obviously understood history. Audi may now have a place on the pantheon of Le Mans contestants, but in 2001 it was still a new boy. Bentley, by contrast, had all the charisma of a great Le Mans name, even if it was now part of the giant German car concern. The name of MG was also hallowed, and both marques returned to Le Mans that year, arguably giving it a glamour that had been lacking in 2000. The Bentley chassis was built in Britain and it was not, as some tried to claim, a green Audi. However, it did use the same 3.6-litre twin-turbo as the R8, although development to work within the LM-GTP rules meant that it had become increasingly dissimilar to the Audi unit.

Despite the newcomers, Audi should have won easily again, and in the event, it did so with a repeat victory for Kristensen, Pirro, and Biela; two down, one more to go for the trio. It was not, however, the cruise to the flag of the previous year, and it was only due to a greater number of delays that the equally quick R8 of Capello, Aiello, and Pescatori did not win on this occasion. All six drivers described the race as their hardest-ever Le Mans.

Only two of the works Joest-run cars were entered this year, but they were backed up by the entries from Johansson Motorsports and Champion Racing, the latter including former three-times Grand Prix victor Johnny Herbert in its line-up. Champion engineer Brad Kettler confessed that team owner Dave Maraj had never heard of the Englishman when he was recommended to the team, despite the fact that, apart from Michele Alboreto, he was the only Formula 1 winner to race an R8.

Both private Audis performed well in qualifying,

Stefan Johansson (Sweden)

One of the most experienced drivers to have raced an R8, Stefan Johansson entered the ELMS, Le Mans and selected ALMS races in 2001 with an Arena-run, Gulf sponsored car. He easily took the European series, having won at Most and then went on to race for Champion in 2002 and at the start of 2003. Having won the British Formula 3 championship in 1980, the Swede progressed to Formula 1, driving for a variety of teams, notably Ferrari and McLaren, and scoring 12 podium places in 88 races. He also competed in CART, running thrice in the Indianapolis 500 during the mid-1990s. In 1996 he returned to sports car racing, winning at Le Mans in 1997 with fellow R8 pilots-to-be, Alboreto and Kristensen, and at Sebring the same year.

finishing in third (Ralph Kelleners in the Champion car) and fifth (Stefan Johansson), to line up behind the works cars with Capello winning the pole. All was not well though. The gearshift paddles played up and new wiring looms had to be manufactured on site. Problem solved.

On the fourth lap of the race, the heavens opened and, until well into the night, spasmodic heavy rain caused nightmarish conditions, and a general feeling that Noah's Ark might be the ideal vehicle to win the race. As darkness fell the conditions were worse than anyone could remember at La Sarthe. Four times the safety car came out, but often the drivers were left alone to battle the conditions, probably more than each other. Following a brilliant start, a slick-shod Aiello spun off shortly after the rain started, bending his rear suspension. Martin Brundle's Bentley led briefly, but any thought that the green coupés could beat the R8s ended with gear selection problems. Biela took over the lead, and from then on he and his team-mate never put a foot wrong as they made their way to the finish.

The customer Audis failed to get past midnight. Johansson was one of those to go off when the initial cloudburst struck. Having lost three laps for repairs, he was on his way back up the field when, during the third hour, his R8's ECU failed. Ralf Kelleners also spun the Champion entry early on but, by the end of the fourth hour, it was up to third place. Co-driver Johnny Herbert then closed down on the second place factory car, and was just three minutes behind when Didier Theys took over. Immediately, their R8's clutch failed and what had become the biggest threat to a Joest one-two was out. Up front, Kristensen was pulling away, but then, during one of Pirro's stints, the tyre pressure sensors indicated a puncture and the other Joest car took over for a brief lead ... only to lose it again once both R8s had changed to high downforce bodywork to cope with the wet. Kristensen had gone on a charge and Aiello had spun at Arnage.

Matters had now really started to go wrong for Aiello's car. Sixth gear failed, meaning a new rear end, a simple under five minute matter thanks to the R8's design. Then the ECU had to be changed, after which Capello spun

Battle damage on Capello's winning car at Sears Point in 2001. (Courtesy Gary Horrocks)

desperately trying to catch up. The car was now three laps down and looking unlikely to overhaul the leader as, up front, Kristensen put in a particularly quick triple stint. However, the drama was not over yet. The Dane was experiencing problems with fourth gear. Changing gear on the straights while not on full throttle, thanks to the standing water, was damaging the gearbox. With just 3½ hours to the finish, he was into that garage and, again, the Audi mechanics made one of their ultra-rapid rear end changes. The car still had a five minute advantage as Pirro took over

and left the pits. The rain gods had not finished yet though, and with two hours left to run, they again did their worst. Out came the safety car, with the Joest cars a lap apart. When the green flags flew, Aiello unlapped himself, but could only pull out about 20 seconds on Pirro. With half an hour to go, he realised that this was a futile task, and allowed himself to be lapped by the Italian, to ensure the cameras would record one of those formation finishes that became such a feature of the Audi R8 years at Le Mans.

"There was not a huge visible difference between the

Portland 2001 has been described as one of the most exiting of all ALMS races. Tom Kristensen (seen here) and Dindo Capello were to be involved in the first half battle, before gearshift problems intervened. (Courtesy Gary Horrocks)

car that started in 2000 and the one that finished in 2006," said Kristensen. "But there were a lot of small, fine detail changes and, of course, the installation of the FSI engine. This was a bonus in two ways during the nightmare, wet race at Le Mans. It was better on fuel economy and had better response; there was not so much turbo lag as in 2000, when there was a wild engine response." Only after the race did Audi admit to the new engine.

Domination on both sides of the Atlantic

The Johansson, and the Joest and Champion teams, now went their separate ways. The Swede was Audi's sole representative in the ELMS. A month after Le Mans, he was joined by Tom Coronel, who had had little chance to drive the car at Le Mans, and Patrick Lemarié, who replaced Guy Smith for financial reasons, for the 1000km race at Estoril. The trio fought for the lead with a Pescarolo, but eventually Coronel was hit from behind by Boris Derichebourg in the French car, and spectacularly spun out of the race. It was the first defeat for an R8 for just over a year. Coronel was unhurt, but Johansson was incensed. Johansson and BAR test driver Lemarié bounced back at Most for an easy, four lap win, the only one for the Gulf-sponsored car. Despite the fact that only the Johansson Audi had entered the final two races, R8 drivers totally dominated the ELMS table, filling the top six places. Johansson, on 123 points, was a dominant winner.

Over in North America, the position was almost as good, with the top four places in the ALMS going to the Audi boys. In this case, it was Emanuele Pirro who emerged as champion. The Audis did not have it all their own way, though. In the six American races that followed Le Mans, they took four victories to Panoz's two. Initially, all went well for the Joest team on its return to the USA. At Sears Point, just over a month after Le Mans, the factory R8s tussled for the entire two and three quarter hours of the race, Capello and Kristensen choosing a better fuel strategy, which saw them just under seven seconds ahead at the end. The Champion car was back in fourth, behind the Panoz of Magnussen and Brabham that was to give the R8s one of the races of their life a few weeks later, at Portland.

That Oregon battle has gone down as one of the most exciting in ALMS history, the lead changing hands during the first half between the Panoz and the Capello/Kristensen Audi with impressive frequency. Forty-five minutes before the end of the 131-lap race, Capello pitted, complaining of gearshift problems, and the car dropped back to fifth. The Biela/Pirro R8, which earlier had fallen back with handling problems, took up the challenge and, at the end, was a mere 0.374 seconds behind the Panoz. Another 15.589 seconds back was the Team Champion entry of Johnny Herbert and Andy Wallace.

Perhaps there was something about Canada that the Audi R8s did not particularly like, but more of them seemed to crash at Mosport than at any other track. In 2001, a damp patch pitched Kristensen and a slick-shod R8-405 into the barriers in the early stages of the race, while Herbert also crashed R8-505 – which was to become the most used and successful of the R8s – 11 laps before the end. Thankfully, Biela and Pirro kept going to finish two laps ahead of that Panoz. Magnussen and Brabham were, though, back on the top step of the podium with their US-built, front-engined car following the next round, a 116-lap affair at Mid-Ohio. This, though, was a race that Audi handed to Panoz, despite the fact that the two Joest cars dominated the proceedings to a point where they held a lap lead by half distance. Full-course yellows negated that advantage; then Capello mistakenly overtook the safety car and was punished with a stop-and-go penalty. A need to change the spark plug coils in the left-hand cylinder block ruined the chances of the other Joest car, the eventual result being that the Joest entries finished second and fourth, the Champion R8, fifth.

The Panoz would not win again in 2001 though, and in the final two rounds of the ALMS, at Laguna Seca and Road Atlanta, R8s secured all three podium places. Both races fell to the Biela/Pirro pairing in R8-503 and both times the Capello/Kristensen car retired, thus giving Pirro the championship. Johansson had chosen to miss the final round of the European series to compete in these races. Again paired with Lemarié, he swapped places with

Champion's Herbert and Wallace over those last two races, finishing in third and second spots respectively.

Kristensen's retirement around half distance at Laguna Seca was arguably remarkable, it being caused by a damaged clutch. In two years of racing, it was the first retirement by a factory R8 that had been caused by a technical problem. Joest would continue to run works R8s until the end of 2003, but it was never to happen again. An examination of the reasons for retirement of all the R8s makes impressive reading. Six DNFs were caused by accidents. Otherwise, there was little that caused an R8 to stop. By far the most disastrous race in terms of mechanical failure was Le Mans in 2001, when as many as two of them, the Champion and Johansson entries, had fallen out with clutch and electrical problems respectively. A year later, the Goh car dropped out of the Suzuka 1000km, also with electrical trouble, when, as the only Le Mans prototype in the field, it should have finished the race an easy winner. The following season, there was the embarrassing debacle of the out-of-fuel Audi

UK car at Le Mans (of which more anon) and otherwise, apart from Kristensen's clutch at Laguna Seca, that was it. Thirteen different Audi R8s (16 cars in total were made by the factory) ran in 80 races, with a total of 180 starts. In all that time, there were only four retirements for technical reasons. It was a truly remarkable record and one that underlines why the Audi R8 must be considered one of the greatest of all endurance racers. It conquered not only its competitors, but also the very length of the events that epitomise sports car racing.

Both Joest teams still had a chance of winning the championship as they went into the final round. However, this time, race leader Kristensen crashed just before the end of the first hour, and that was it as far as the title was concerned. It had been a season of 'two halves,' with the yellow highlighted car dominating the first half, and the red the second.

The main difference in the results of those final two races was that the two customer teams swapped places,

Pierre Kaffer (Germany)

German, Pierre Kaffer won exactly half of his eight races with an R8, most notable of which was the Sebring 12 Hours. The former Formula 3 driver only contested the 2004 season with the car, racing for Audi Sport UK Team Veloqx and then, for the last two ALMS rounds, for Champion. He stayed with the marque for 2005 and 2006, racing for Audi Sport Team Joest in the DTM, before moving into GT2 with success in a Ferrari F430.

The 2001 season was the first in which privateer Audis fought with the works cars. (Courtesy Gulf)

the Champion car, resplendent in new reflective livery, coming home second in California, the Johansson one second in Georgia. Both had performed well, Champion having come close to its first victory, only to be thwarted when Johnny Herbert picked up a twenty second penalty following a collision with that Panoz, the only car to have troubled the R8s all season. The Englishman was still only 1.602 seconds behind at the finish, but Champion boss Dave Maraj would have to wait until mid-2003 for that first win with an R8. After that, they would fall thick and fast. At Road Atlanta both customer cars led at some stage, but stop-and-go penalties, wheel damage and malfunctioning lighting dropped them back.

The America Le Mans Series appeared healthy but there did not seem to be enough support for its new European counterpart. The latter was dropped, and that meant an end for Johansson's R8 programme with Gulf. The Swede had seen this as more a long-term relationship and was disappointed that it would not be allowed to 'blossom.' The iconic blue and orange colours would next be seen on Courage and Zytek LMP2s, and then on works Aston Martins. The oil company's association with Audi had been brief.

So ended 2001, with the Audi R8 firmly established as dominant top dog, despite being in only its second season. The year 2002 and March's Sebring 12 Hours loomed, and that was a race the R8 was never to lose.

2002 – Audi R8
Achieving the hat-trick

If a manufacturer would choose to dominate one endurance event other than the Le Mans 24 Hours, it would surely be Sebring. The classic event, on the remote Florida airfield from where Boeing B17s – including the famed 'Memphis Belle' – once took off, was the first to count for the World Sports Car Championship when that series commenced in 1953. Twelve hours in length, its duration is currently second only to La Sarthe for the Le Mans prototypes, and it also resonates with the US public.

The Audi R8 was even more successful on Sebring's concrete than at Le Mans, remaining unbeaten there throughout its six years. The year 2002 was no exception. Despite left rear suspension damage caused by a collision early in the race, Dindo Capello, Johnny Herbert, and Christian Pescatori in a new, Joest-entered chassis, came home a lap ahead of Champion's faithful R8-505. The second factory car, with which Biela had taken the pole, was also involved in a collision that ensured it was back in fifth place at the end. Prior to being chopped by a Porsche, the Biela/Capello/Kristensen car had been in contention. After that, the previous two years' Le Mans winning crew had nothing but troubles.

For Herbert, who had won Le Mans for Mazda in 1991, it was a particularly pleasing victory. Andy Wallace reckoned that he, Stefan Johansson, and Jan Lammers, had "... driven our nuts off" for 12 hours, but their second place Champion R8 could never stay with the works entries. The factory said that its cars, R8-601 and R8-602, were just tidied-up versions of the 2001 R8. Champion begged to differ and said that the host of small revisions made added up to a significant improvement over its car. Wallace said that

Andy Wallace "drove the nuts off" the Champion Racing car at Sebring in 2002. (Courtesy Gary Horrocks)

the factory cars were 2½ seconds quicker around Sebring. "It's just bloody difficult. We simply can't match the factory cars on speed, much less make up time, particularly when we're having to pass seven or eight slower cars every lap," said the Oxford-born driver at the time. Reflecting back, he reckons that a private entry is only ever there "... to pick up the pieces when things go wrong" for the factory cars. He was to find exactly the same thing later in the decade when driving Dyson Racing-entered Porsche Spyder LMP2s against the Penske factory versions.

Two months later, that annoying Panoz pairing of Magnussen and Brabham took the flag ahead of the Audis. On only five occasions between the start of the 2000 season and July 2003 was Audi beaten in an ALMS race, and each

Tom Kristensen (Denmark)

Five times the R8 won at Le Mans, five times Tom Kristensen was at the wheel. All the more remarkable is the fact that in the year the R8 did not come home first, the watch-collecting Dane was driving the winning Bentley. He also won the race in 1997 in Joest's TWR-Porsche and then, again with Audi, in the diesel era, making him easily the most successful driver at La Sarthe. In all, Kristensen took 17 victories from his 31 starts in the Audi, those in 2002 taking him to the ALMS championship. Prior to his time in sports cars, he had won both the German and Japanese Formula 3 championships and, in 1996, finished sixth in the Formula 3000 championship.

time it was the Danish/Australian duo in a Panoz. Their names should undoubtedly be remembered in the annals of the R8 alongside those of the Audi regulars. Perhaps Sears Point, which during 2002 changed its name, in corporate fashion, to Infinion Raceway, had something against the R8s, for it was here that Audi was to be beaten in an ALMS race for the first time by anything other than a Panoz.

The 2002 race was one of torrential rain and plenty of drama, as Herbert and Kristensen finished a mere 0.482 seconds behind the Panoz in the Champion car, the Englishman going sideways across the finishing line. The result meant that Herbert, who had given up the chance of qualifying for the Indianapolis 500 with Duesenberg Brothers Racing's Dallara to honour his contract with Champion, had opened up a nine point lead in the ALMS championship. With Le Mans looming, the factory rolled out R8-405 for the final appearance of a 2000-build car. Down the field following an earlier spin by Capello, Pirro was involved in a 'racing accident' when being lapped by Magnussen, causing the pole-sitting R8 to leave the track in spectacular fashion, although it soldiered on to finish 15th following a rear-end change.

Le Mans

Le Mans 2002 was all about the threes for the factory Audis – first three positions on the grid, first three positions at the finish, and a third consecutive win from Tom Kristensen, Frank Biela, and Emmanuel Pirro. For the third year running, the Audi R8s were clear favourites to win and the drivers were allowed to fight amongst themselves for victory. The two Joest cars responded with a great duel, the winners, like the previous year, having fewer problems than the defeated. For the first time an Audi also led for every lap of the 24 hour race.

Following 2001's appalling conditions, it was scorching at Le Mans for 2002. Dindo Capello took the pole, and new to the factory team Johnny Herbert took advantage of this, holding the lead in its car at the start, despite a determined attempt by Biela to seize the advantage at the Dunlop Chicane. Nobody else seemed to get a look in. Herbert held the lead to the first pit stops, but then it changed back-and-forth a number of times. Fear of a puncture meant that the tyres on Herbert's car were changed at the second stop. Not wanting to waste time by swapping drivers at the next stop, and then tyres at the fourth instead of both at the same time,

The hat-trick got Pirro out of his seat at Le Mans. (Courtesy Audi)

meant the Englishman was to stay in his R8 for a massive four stints. In all, he was to be at the wheel for 11 of the 24 hours. The eventual second place was scant reward for the 1991 winner.

Audi's precaution with Herbert's tyres was well founded, as Kristensen in the other Joest car became the first of the Audi drivers to suffer a puncture. Then, Pescatori, who had taken over from Herbert, had a blow out and lost a lap as he nursed the car back to the pits. Matters were made worse by a second stop immediately after this, for a precautionary front tyre change to improve the car's balance. Now the

car was well behind its stable mate. Herbert, Pescatori, and Capello chased hard. Kristensen punctured again and Herbert briefly got back on the lead lap. However, punctures were now becoming the order of the day – a change to the gravel traps was blamed – and the second-placed car suffered two more in the tenth and 18th hours, one of them particularly frightening for Capello. Now the Audi North America-entered R8 of Michael Krumm, Philipp Peter, and Marco Werner was becoming a threat. This had suffered the first of the punctures – on the parade lap – and had been forced to start the race last. However, the car was

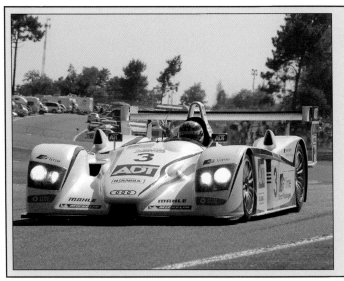

JJ Lehto (Finland)

Another double-figure winner with the R8, the rapid JJ Lehto took 14 wins from 31 starts. He has been described as easily the most successful non-factory driver of the car, having driven for Champion between 2003 and 2005, twice winning the ALMS title during this period. Only Tom Kristensen scored more fastest laps with the R8, racking up 12 to the Finn's ten. The British Formula 3 champion in 1988, Lehto went on to start 62 Grands Prix with a variety of teams, but only finished on the podium once. After a spell in the DTM he moved into sports car racing. His winning drive during the night at Le Mans, in a McLaren in 1995, was the stuff of legend. He also competed in the CART single seater series in North America during 1998 before racing, initially for BMW, in the ALMS.

eventually to suffer from electrical problems meaning the drivers were never able to improve on third place.

At the front, though, there was drama again, as the lead car refused to fire up following a routine stop at about 10.30am. Five minutes were lost in the garage. Eventually, Biela was able to leave the pits just as Herbert exited Mulsanne corner, less than a lap behind. However, the lead crept back to over a lap, although Herbert was again able to unlap himself just before the end, before falling back again for the formation finish. As they had done in 2000, the three silver cars with, respectively, their red, yellow, and black trim, crossed the line together. Pirro, perhaps typically, gave his engine enough revs to even climb up on his seat as he crossed the line. Nobody had been able to live with the Audis throughout the entire 24 Hours. It could even have been a one-two-three-four, but the fourth R8, Team Goh's year old car, spent 25 minutes in the pits with cooling troubles and could only finish in seventh. Team owner Kazimuchi Goh recalled, later, that his car seemed to be having problems every hour. The third successive win meant that Audi could now keep the Le Mans trophy, and it was taken off to display in the company's museum at Ingolstadt.

Achieving the hat-trick, said Wolfgang Ullrich, had justified Audi's decision to go sports car racing. It had given Audi the sense of heritage that it wanted to achieve in just four short years. He pointed out that it had been endurance racing that had originally established sporting images for many car manufacturers, not Formula 1, and that had been a factor that had driven Audi's programme.

Kristensen, Biela, and Pirro were a unique combination, able to set up the car for each other and needing little seat adjustment during driver changes. They rarely made mistakes, and while luck may have played a certain part in the way that they habitually beat their team-mates at Le Mans, there is no doubting that they deserved their historic hat-trick. With such a record achieved, Ullrich went on record to say that he thought it no longer important for Audi to enter a factory team for Le Mans, and that the Volkswagen Audi Group was looking at a number of options. As far as he was concerned, whatever happened, it would be a shame to pension off the R8s. The factory may have been about to stop racing them as far as the 24 hour race was concerned, but their story there was far from over.

Mainly America

By contrast to Le Mans, Mid-Ohio was a mere bagatelle, short enough for Capello and Kristensen to attempt to run the race with just a single fuel stop. With one lap left to go, the Dane was still ahead of Pirro in the other Joest car. Then the fuel ran out, and with just 300 metres to go the Italian swept past. By means of its starter motor, the erstwhile leader staggered over the line in second place.

The Joest pair was still at it a couple of weeks later at Road America, swapping the lead for the entire 4¼ hours. A couple of stop-and-go penalties for Capello looked as if the result might be a repeat of Mid-Ohio, but then tyre failure for the Pirro/Biela car handed victory back to its rival. By finishing on the same lap, despite Johansson's excursion through a gravel trap, the Champion car ensured Audi's first ALMS one-two-three of the season.

The Panoz repeated its Sears Point performance, with another sub-one second victory at Washington, the Capello/Kristensen car having been given another of those stop-and-go penalties. Biela and Pirro also lost time due to a safety car period, but were still third, only 8.701 seconds behind the winner at the finish.

From now on, Audi would win all the remaining rounds of the championship, with Kristensen taking the title. It was back to one-two-three at Trois-Rivières for the next round. The difference on this occasion was that, with qualifying cut short, Kristensen and Capello had to start from 20th spot on the grid, but with Pirro and Biela's pit strategy going astray in the later stages of the race, they still won. For the second Canadian encounter, Mosport, the pair continued their fight until Pirro slid off the track and slammed into a tyre wall. The Italian was taken to hospital for a checkup and the Champion R8 inherited second place, a lap behind the winner.

Tom Kristensen (seen here) and Johnny Herbert finished a mere 0.482 seconds behind the winning Panoz at Sears Point. (Courtesy Gary Horrocks)

At Sears Point, Emanuele Pirro left the track in spectacular fashion ... (Courtesy Gary Horrocks)

... but the car soldiered on to finish 15th. (Courtesy Gary Horrocks)

The Panoz was the only car capable of beating the R8s in America during 2002. The race at Washington was one such example. (Courtesy Gary Horrocks)

Patrick Lemarié (France)

Patrick Lemarié replaced Guy Smith in Stefan Johansson's car for Le Mans and the latter part of the 2001 season. In all, he drove the Gulf R8 on five occasions, winning at Most. The previous year he had made his Le Mans debut driving an LMP675 Debora. The Parisian, a friend of Jacques Villeneuve, was a tester for the Formula 1 BAR team, and spent a couple of years in Formula 3000 before driving for PK Racing in CART during the first six races of the 2003 season

Biela and Pirro led the whole way at Laguna Seca 2002. (Courtesy Gary Horrocks)

Following a light collision, the rear right suspension track rod was changed on the second Joest car at Laguna Seca, dropping it back to fourth at the finish. (Courtesy Gary Horrocks)

Despite having been momentarily unconscious, Pirro was unharmed in the accident and back on form for Laguna Seca, where he and Biela led from the pole to the chequered flag. Herbert and Johansson reprieved their Mosport second place when a collision dropped the other factory car back to fourth. The postponed race on the streets of Miami saw another win for the German/Italian pairing, although there was something new about this win; the pair used just one set of tyres for the 122-lap race. More stop-and-go penalties affected the result though, with Joest denied a one-two when Kristensen was awarded a penalty with less than eight minutes to go. The Champion car was punished in like manner, resulting in these two cars finishing third and fifth, a Cadillac splitting the works cars on the podium for the first and only time.

The Petit Le Mans 1000 mile race at Road Atlanta

once again concluded the ALMS season. Kristensen and Capello drove to a convincing win over the Georgia track's undulations, thus securing the drivers title for the Dane. It was revenge for the 'yellow' car. Sixth place was a poor finale for the other Joest Audi, after Pirro had been unable to avoid a burning car that had braked suddenly in front of him. Herbert and Johansson in Champion's R8-505 were just under a minute behind the works car in second place. The R8's dominance of the ALMS was earning it the nickname of the 'Panzer' in North America.

There is just one other 2002 race to take note of, a unique event in the story of the Audi R8, in that the one entered was the only Le Mans prototype in the field and, thus, even more of a favourite to win than usual. Pole position was a formality. Ironically, due to electronic problems, Seiji Ara and Hiroki Katoh did not finish the Suzuka 1000km in R8-501, which had been entered, as at Le Mans, by the Japanese Goh team. Thus, for the only time in its history, an Audi R8 was beaten by, of all things, a Toyota Supra. Team Goh's hour was yet to come.

Kristensen leads Pirro at Petit Le Mans, on his way to securing the ALMS Drivers' Championship. (Courtesy Gary Horrocks)

2003 – Audi R8
Sole Le Mans defeat

As the Volkswagen Group's focus, with support from Joest, was firmly on victory for Bentley at Le Mans, the emphasis, as far as the R8 was concerned, turned to private entries, albeit ones connected to national distributors. Joining the existing American Champion outfit and the Japanese Team Goh was Audi Sport UK, which purchased R8-603, the only previous outing for this car having been at Le Mans the year before, when it came third in factory hands. Driven by Jonny Kane, Perry McCarthy, and Miko Salo, and run that first year by Mike Earle's Arena squad, this joined Champion's R8-505 and what was now the sole Joest entry of R8-604 for Audi's annual domination of Sebring.

The UK squad was a true 'dream come true' for its team manager, David Ingram. He had already seen how the R8 had followed on from the quattro in creating an exciting identity for Audi. "When I started with Audi we were just an anonymous German car company. Some people in Britain were not even aware that the company was German."

Ingram confessed he had been obsessed with Le Mans since he first went there in 1982 as a spectator, and then as a refueller for Richard Lloyd's Porsche 956. Not missing a year, he noted that there was the odd Audi in the car parks at La Sarthe, "but not many." He progressed to being project manager for Audi UK's touring car race programme, and in 1997 received the first inkling that his employer would be taking on the race that was his real love. "A couple of years before we went there I discovered that, as a brand, we were thinking of going to Le Mans. I made it my business to support this with as much enthusiasm but I did not know how we would take to Le Mans. This was big time motor racing."

In 2003, David Ingram realised a dream; running a team at Le Mans. (Author's collection)

Allan McNish (Scotland)

It is a travesty that Allan McNish, who has put in some of the great drives of sports car history, did not win Le Mans in an R8, the Scot's two victories having come prior to the Audi era, and then in the time of the diesels. In 2000 he was the most successful of the Audi team, winning the ALMS. However, while his former colleagues were racking up victories at Le Mans, he decamped to Formula 1, with Toyota. He returned in 2004 with Team Veloqx, bravely bringing his badly crashed car back to the pits that year at Le Mans, before collapsing with concussion. It is a matter of pride to McNish that he was in the winning car at Lime Rock in 2006, the final appearance of an R8.

The Champion Racing entry led for much of Sebring 2003, but it would be another two years before the American team won the race. (Courtesy Gary Horrocks)

He had observed that the touring car programme was starting to add "excitement" to the Audi brand. "We saw the success that touring cars gave us and wanted to step up a league. It was fundamentally the same personalities and even some of the drivers. We were going into the big boys racing."

He continued: "It has been interesting to see the difference in the audience's attitude. A different dynamic was developing in the Audi image. The enthusiasts who did not see Audi as that type of a brand beforehand could see something developing.

"You could almost feel the enthusiasm for Audi increase as our list of successes at Le Mans grew. The number of Audis in the car park certainly increased. We used the R8 to inspire some of the thinking behind the road cars. The same passion was going into the road cars. Before the Le Mans programme it would not have been thinkable for us to produce the R8 road car. It would have been a step too far for the brand. That credibility cascades down the range."

Audi UK had been taking guests to Le Mans prior to 2003. In what Ingram now describes as a flash of

Marco Werner, and team-mates, inherited the lead at Sebring, just 90 minutes before the end of the 12 hour race.
(Courtesy Gary Horrocks)

inspiration, its director at the time, Kevin Rose, inquired about the possibility of it running its own car there. "The timing," said Ingram, "was perfect. The Bentley programme was coming up to its third year and there were a lot of resources from the group going into that. One of the by-products of this was that Audi decided not to run a works team in 2003 so this was our opportunity. I spoke to the people I knew in Audi Sport from touring car days. We came to an agreement whereby we could buy a car and I put together a programme. In normal circumstances we would have gone straight to Richard Lloyd [who had run the R8Cs as the Audi UK touring cars] but he was involved in the Bentley project. A suitable alternative was found in the person of Mike Earle who had run the Johansson R8. The logic was that his guys understood the R8. We decided to do Sebring as a warm up and then Le Mans. For me

Mika Salo, a veteran of 109 Grands Prix, was one of the drivers for the new Audi Sport UK entry.
(Courtesy Gary Horrocks)

personally it was magnificent. I had gone very quickly from being an enthusiastic spectator to project managing a team at Le Mans."

The Audi UK R8 tale did not, though, begin under the Florida sun, but rather on a typically cold winter's day at Snetterton, Norfolk, when the team, along with drivers Mika Salo, Perry McCarthy, and Jonny Kane gathered for the first time. Finn Salo was surprised to find how easy the car was to drive, even in what were tricky conditions. The

mechanics were also finding it was a great car to work on.

It was, however, the American-entered R8 of Champion Racing that led for much of Sebring's 12 hour race, before a full-course yellow and an unscheduled pit stop with just 90 minutes to go handed victory to the Joest car again, driven on this occasion by Frank Biela, Philipp Peter, and Marco Werner. German, Werner had joined Audi the previous year for Le Mans, going on to win a total of 14 races in an R8. For Austrian Peter, who had also been his team-mate in the 24 Hours, it was to be the second and final race in such a car. Stefan Johansson, JJ Lehto, and Emanuele Pirro were just over 13 seconds behind at the finish for Champion; one of the closest ever finishes at Sebring. The American team must have been wondering just when it would win a round of the ALMS, although there were some who said that its unusual tactics, changing its planned sequence of drivers during the full-course yellow, meant that it only had itself to blame. However, there were peculiar circumstances that day, including the fact that Pirro had leg cramp and had to make an unscheduled stop.

"It was really demoralising. We just did not seem to be able to win a race," said Champion's chief engineer Brad Kettler. "We did everything right, had good results everywhere but we just did not seem able to close the deal. It was a frustrating time."

Newcomer Audi UK finished sixth after a series of annoying delays. The 2002-spec car had not enjoyed the race pace of its sister R8s, although Northern Ireland's Kane had been within two-tenths of Pirro in qualifying. Earle pointed out that his team had only been working with the Audi for a few weeks, unlike the years of the Joest and Champion Racing squads, and that, at the beginning of practice, the team had been as much as two seconds slower

Stéphane Ortelli (France)

Stéphane Ortelli was one of the first factory R8 drivers in 2000, but only raced such a car on six occasions – in that year and in 2005, when he made a comeback with the ORECA team. It was during that second season that he scored his only R8 win, when, teamed with Allan McNish at Silverstone, he scored fastest lap in the closing stages to help secure a famous victory. It was also with McNish that he scored his only victory at Le Mans, driving a Porsche 911 GT in 1998. Since his time with the R8, Ortelli has scored success in the GT classes. His spectacular 2008 crash at Monza in an LMP1 Courage was one of those that highlighted a danger at the time; that of LMP cars taking off. Coincidentally, he narrowly missed the Audi R10 of one Allan McNish.

Powered by an Audi engine and with the R8C as an ancestor, the Bentley Speed 8 was the only car ever to beat the R8 at Le Mans. (Author's collection)

The Audi Sport UK entry did not get much further than this at Le Mans in 2003. (Author's collection)

than the quick cars. Now, Kane was almost as quick as one of the three time Audi R8 Le Mans winners.

The year 2003 had begun in the same way as 2002 had finished. With the Bentleys third and fourth in their only race outside of France, it was a total walkover for the Volkswagen Audi Group. A recalcitrant clutch and a collision that resulted in a rear end change for the UK R8, prevented a clean sweep of the top five. Even that was punctuated by just one Panoz. At one point, Salo had mightily harried Kristensen in one of the new Bentley Speed 8s. It should, however, be pointed out that the Bentleys driven by R8 veterans Herbert and Capello had been first and second in qualifying, only to be sent to the back of the grid when their rear diffusers had been found to be fractionally too high. Perhaps that was the writing on the wall, for, from one classic event, the teams travelled to another three months later, and what was to be the only really significant race that the Audi R8 was not to win – the 2003 Le Mans 24 Hours. In the meantime, the Audi UK car went back to Snetterton for further testing.

Le Mans

The year 2003 will be remembered as the one when the Audi R8 did not come first at Le Mans. There were those who wondered whether the Volkswagen Group would order the three national Audi teams to allow the Bentleys (now in their third year of a three-year programme) the first victory for the marque since 1930. The teams emphatically denied this at a jovial pre-race press conference – "it was an out-and-out battle between us," Ingram recalled later – but, even so, the R8s could not live with the pair of green coupés. The Audis seemed to have only one advantage, their fuel consumption – in the early stages of the race they could go 16 laps to the Bentleys' 13 – and it was not enough.

During the May 4 test day, Frank Biela – who had replaced Jonny Kane in the Audi UK R8 – went off on oil damaging the back end. Annoyingly, yellow flags came out immediately after to indicate said oil. Ingram consoled Biela; it was one of those things.

The Audi cause was not helped when, early in the race, Biela in the British car – which had appeared the quickest of the R8s – failed to negotiate a slower Panoz when trying to enter the pits. With only $3\frac{1}{2}$ litres fuel left, insufficient for another $8\frac{1}{2}$-mile lap, and despite weaving to pick up the last dregs, Biela's R8 ground to a halt at Indianapolis. "It's over," he said on the radio, followed by something choice in German. "Drive on the starter motor and switch the lights off," he was told, and he forced the car to hiccup away again, but it came to a final stop after Arnage, less than two miles from home. With refuelling only allowed in the pits, the British entry's race was over.

A film crew, making a documentary about Audi Sport UK's Le Mans, was forced to rethink, and produced what is probably the only film about Le Mans that was mainly shot at Sebring. Ingram recalled: "It just was not real, it was not happening. It hit me for six." He would be back; Le Mans had become unfinished business. Biela had been drafted-in to provide experience, none of Audi UK's drivers at Sebring having raced an R8 before this season. However, over in the

First R8 home at Le Mans but, for once, not the winner; the Champion entry rounds Indianapolis corner (Author's collection)

Bentley pit, Kane, now reserve driver for the British Racing Green coupés, was disappointed to see his old car go out so early. Nothing more to do, some of the UK team took themselves off to a free Jamiroquai concert taking place inside the circuit.

The Bentleys had, anyway, shot off into the distance and had almost a minute in hand over the three Audis at the end of the first hour. The two coupés were some three seconds a lap faster than the German cars. The Japanese entry was the leading R8 for most of the first five hours. The Champion car, whose fluorescent livery shone out, then took over and, despite being delayed by a bonnet change in the late evening, remained in third place. A few hours later, the Goh R8 had to stop for ten minutes due to a fuel injection problem. A chasing Dome closed to within two laps, but did not threaten seriously before falling back with electrical problems. In the late morning Lehto, in

the Champion R8, had a brief off-course excursion but sustained no damage.

The two R8s stayed in third and fourth for the rest of the race, mirroring the R8R's result in 1999. It was easily the R8's worst Le Mans and it was not to happen again.

Back to normal

It was job done for Bentley. The menacing green cars were never to race again and, 23 days after Le Mans, it was back to situation normal for the Audi R8 at a hot and humid Road Atlanta. Positions were, though, reversed from Sebring, as Lehto, from third place on the grid, overtook Werner in the first corner, going on to win by over 30 seconds with Johnny Herbert, the Englishman back from Bentley duties. Two years and 17 top-five finishes since it had entered the series with an R8, Dave Maraj's team had, at last, won an ALMS round. "We were better just right off the truck," recalled Brad Kettler. "We were quicker in every practice. JJ and Johnny were working well together. They just took off and we led the race early. It was what we needed."

It had taken Champion Racing a long time to beat the factory. At the end of the previous season Kettler had come close to resigning, such was his frustration. However, as he was now to say: "Once we had done it, we were able to do it again and again."

It was to be the first of two wins for the Champion car that year at Road Atlanta, the victory in June's 128-lapper being followed up in October by another at the 394-lap Petit Le Mans. Before then there occurred Audi's second defeat of the season, in what was only the fourth race. It was to be the last time that the R8 was beaten that year, though. At Sears Point, the lighter Lola EX257 (using an MG-badged AER engine) of James Weaver and Butch Leitzinger, entered in the LMP675 class and fought a race-long battle with the Joest and Champion cars. With just three laps left, less than a second separated the Dyson Racing Lola from Werner in the Joest R8. However, the German lost time lapping a GT, leaving the Lola to finish 3.7 seconds ahead. Thirty-six seconds further back, Herbert just snatched third place in the final corner from a Lista-entered Dallara-MG, following a late tyre change.

The rest of the North American season was a matter of Biela and Werner winning in Joest's R8-604, or Herbert and Lehto coming first in Champion's R8-505. The former took victory in both the Canadian races, Trois-Rivières and Mosport. Pit stop strategy was crucial in the first of these, as the German car finished a relatively easy winner over the American. At Mosport, Champion Racing was more competitive but ultimately less successful; a race-long duel was ended 19 minutes from the end when Herbert collided with a GT car, damaging R-505's right-hand suspension, meaning that it was only classified in 20th place.

Herbert and Lehto bounced back at Road America, for Audi's 30th overall ALMS win. The Joest Audi failed to fire up after the first fuel stop, and the resulting seven-minute starter motor change dropped it back to an ultimate seventh place. The two teams continued to trade wins, Joest

Team Goh's hour was yet to come. In 2003, its car, seen here at Arnage, was fourth. (Author's collection)

taking Laguna Seca, where the Champion car dropped from second to 24th following a precautionary rear end change when the gearbox started to make strange noises, only to carve its way back to fourth. At Miami, Champion risked all by not making a final fuel stop and hoping for a full-course yellow. The gamble worked, and there was still fuel in the tank when it crossed the line just over 40 seconds ahead of the Joest car. Biela and Werner still led the ALMS drivers' championship, though, with one round to go. A third place at Petit Le Mans secured that title, although an early accident initially dropped the pair right down the field. The car also spent time in a gravel trap in the eighth hour, as Herbert and Lehto went on to win by eight laps.

Brad Kettler was to say that some of the best days he had as race engineer were with the Finn – who drove for Champion for thee years – on the other end of the radio. Dave Maraj had watched JJ race a Cadillac in the US, and knew he wanted him in an R8. Kettler was able to introduce a number of drivers to the car, usually in testing at the little, mosquito-infested Moroso Park (now Palm Beach International) circuit. "Almost universally they said the same thing. They came in,

For the first time the Petit Le Mans race at Road Atlanta fell to Champion Racing ... and by eight laps.
(Courtesy Gary Horrocks)

flipped the visor up and said 'now I understand'. They could not believe just how good it really was." However, Lehto also wanted to understand the technical side of the car, the relationships between the various components "and how it all fitted together." The feeling for him was very important. He wanted to feel movement in the carcass of the tyre, but nothing in the car itself.

Team Goh's R8-602 took part in a couple of races in Europe, other than the Le Mans 24 Hours, winning both. Typical, wet Spa conditions saw a first hour battle between Tom Kristensen in the Japanese-entered car and Andy Wallace in the DBA-Zytek. However, Kristensen and Seiji Ara were able to pull away to win the newly revived 1000km classic by four laps. The car returned to Le Mans in the November for a foretaste of the new Le Mans Series, held over the shorter Bugatti circuit. Kristensen and Ara were in a different class from the rest of the field and led throughout.

Sears Point in 2003 was the first time that the Audi R8s had been beaten in North America by anything other than a Panoz. Biela and Werner, in the Joest car, lost out to Dyson Racing's lighter LMP675 Lola. (Courtesy Gary Horrocks)

Marco Werner rounds the Laguna Seca Corkscrew, 2003. (Courtesy Gary Horrocks)

2004 – Audi R8
Fighting on two fronts

For the final two, complete seasons of its life, the Audi R8 fought on two fronts. A new, mainly European-based championship had sprung up, the Le Mans Endurance Series, backed by Le Mans 24 Hours organisers, the ACO. Unlike the American Le Mans Series, this was originally intended to cater only for classic 1000km races. While rounds at such places as Monza, Spa, Silverstone, and even the Nürburgring (though no longer used the formidable Nordschleife), certainly had history, there were LMS races in the coming years at what could hardly be called 'classic' tracks. There had also been a change in the regulations in that the LMP900 class (in which the R8 had been entered) and the LMP675 category had been brought together under the LMP1 banner, it being felt that the performance difference between the two had converged. A new, second class had been introduced, LMP2. In theory, the cars in this category, which was intended for privateers, should have been totally subservient to the LMP1s. In Europe this remained the case. However, Audi was to find that this was not so in North America when, at the end of the following season, Porsche, perhaps against the spirit of the LMP2 rules, introduced its Spyder.

The entry for the first race of the New Year – as usual the Sebring 12 Hours – combined both fronts in that two of the three Audis in the race were entered by Audi UK's new team, the Sam Li run Veloqx operation having replaced Arena. (Veloqx had teamed with Prodrive to win the GTS class at Le Mans the previous year, with a Ferrari.) As a dress rehearsal for Le Mans, it was to be Veloqx's only foray into the US, but it was to result in the two purple and silver cars – arguably the most attractive colour scheme to grace

an R8 – finishing first and third, sandwiching Champion's now ageing R8-505.

David Ingram recalled: "After the unfortunate 2003, Le Mans was unfinished business. Some elements of Audi UK had lost enthusiasm but I was determined. I had to work hard internally. Dr Ullrich had a conversation with Sam Li. He was keen on winning Le Mans and had been running GT Ferraris there. We struck a deal whereby we would jointly run a two-car team to enter at Sebring, in the LMES and at Le Mans. One car was our own from 2003 and Sam brought the other car, which he retains to this day. We would try not to cut corners. It was a significant step up from 2003. It made the year go very quickly. The fact that there was not a works team then made it realistic but I can't see it being repeated."

At Sebring it was R8-603, Audi Sport UK's own car, that won, almost opponent free after the first four hours, driven by Frank Biela, impressive sports car rookie Pierre Kaffer, and Allan McNish, the Scot having returned from Formula 1. The Champion car of JJ Lehto, Emanuele Pirro, and Marco Werner was the first of the other two R8s to hit trouble when impact damage repairs cost it nine laps. Two hours later the second Veloqx car driven by Jamie Davies, Johnny Herbert, and Guy Smith suffered an oil seal failure on the left-side drive shaft. The complete rear end replacements, that had been such a feature of a number of R8 pits stops, had now been outlawed, much to designer Wolfgang Appel's disgust, and the British team now lost 35 minutes replacing a gear plate. McNish now reckoned he could ease off to the flag, with the Champion R8 five laps back at the end and the Audi UK car a further seven. "It was

Christian Pescatori (Italy)

Christian Pescatori raced an Audi R8 on just three occasions, but still scored a victory with the car. Born in the Mille Miglia start and finish town of Brescia, Pescatori was Italian Formula 3 champion in 1993 before progressing to Formula 3000. In 2000 he shared the Sports Racing World Cup with David Terrien, driving a Ferrari 333SP, following this the next season with the N-GT class of the FIA GT Championship. Further GT success came in 2005 with the GTS class of the LMES. It was as a replacement for Michel Alboreto that Pescatori first raced an R8, coming second both that year and in 2002. His win came earlier that second season at Sebring.

a race I've always wanted to win," declared McNish, who had been out of sports car racing for three years. It was not to be his last.

McNish noted: "The driving of the car changed over the years. When I came back in 2004 it had the FSI direct injection. This smoothed out the engine power massively. In the wet we did not have to change the mappings. You could really drive progressively on the throttle. Aerodynamically the car was much less sensitive, mechanically as well. There were two or three drivers who could drive the R8 fast over a long period and in different conditions. There were probably ten drivers who could drive it in 2004."

Audi Sport UK's second car was R8-604, used by Joest the previous year. Joest was no longer on the scene, as it was preparing for the diesel age, leaving Champion, with the exception of Sebring, to contest the ALMS alone, while Veloqx and Goh competed in the LMS, all three teams coming together for Le Mans, itself.

The purple and silver R8s returned to Europe where they were joined by the Goh car for the first round of the new Le Mans Endurance Series, as it was initially known. This was a true classic in that it was the Monza 1000kms, a race on an historic circuit just north of Milan that was first held in the mid-1960s, but had not been run since 2001. It was another one-two-three for the Audis, who seemed to have no real rivals that year, losing just once at Mosport, in August. The fact that in North America only one R8 was campaigned on a regular basis makes this record all the more impressive. At Monza, the two British cars staged a race-long battle, Jamie Davies and Johnny Herbert's car rounding the Parabolica on the last lap a whisker ahead of that of Kaffer and McNish. However, a new challenger had arisen to the R8s. There is a story that, during this race, McNish radioed back to his pit that he could not shift the works Zytek 04S from his tail: recall this to members of the Zytek team, and they will smile and tell you that their car had lost its brakes. The Zytek was to challenge the Audis during Le Mans qualifying and then beat them to the pole at Silverstone.

Meanwhile at Monza, the Goh entry with its three

drivers was hampered by a ride height problem, and just could not keep up with the flying Veloqx cars. An overtaking manoeuvre by Herbert on Kaffer during the race was described as "... inspirational." The pair was baulked by a slower car into the Ascari Chicane, but the Englishman took to the grass on the exit to take the lead.

The race was unusual in that, for the rest of the season, the McNish/Kaffer car was the quicker of the two British entries. Throughout the European season the British R8s also had the measure of the Japanese one, the consistent Dindo Capello perhaps missing partnering a McNish or Kristensen, and Seiji Ara failing to impress. However, there was one very notable exception.

Le Mans

With the Bentley programme over, the Audi R8s were again the favourites to continue where they had left off in 2002. In preliminary practice for the race, Allan McNish achieved a fastest lap of three minutes 32.615 seconds, over five seconds under that of the quickest Audi the previous year. Given that the only changes to the R8 were to the side pods and a narrower rear wing, there was, admitted Audi, just one reason for the considerable improvemen; the tyres. Michelin's circuit racing programme manager Matthieu Bonardel remarked: "Winning every year is not a reason for not improving."

Again, Audi left it to the national teams to represent the marque, as it would do until the advent of the diesel R10 in 2006. The Veloqx duo were first and second on the grid, but were made to work for their places by a sole Zytek 04S, which held pole position for around an hour of qualifying. Zytek's founder Bill Gibson observed that Audi had never been pushed like this before in qualifying for the 24 hours, and it is certain that the British Audi team had to make a major effort to ensure pole position, a motivated Johnny Herbert scoring his first since 1988. The American and Japanese entries qualified behind the Zytek. Audi UK's two engineers, Chris Gorne and Graham Taylor, acknowledged how they had been made to work by the Zytek and were not sure how the new regulations left the R8. According to Taylor, it was "... quite boring – there's not enough development to keep it exciting." A series of restrictions for this season had caused a number of changes to

Lull before the storm: Le Mans 2004.
(Courtesy Tim Wagstaff)

"Now, don't bend it," may be what engineer Graham Taylor is telling Allan McNish before the start of the 2004 Le Mans. (Author's collection)

An Audi R8's clothing. (Author's collection)

Allan McNish (8) and Jamie Davies (88) about to trade paint as they start to race. There is only another 24 hours to go. (Author's collection)

the Audis. The capacity of the fuel cell had been reduced to 80-litres, and the width of the pure element of the wing reduced from 2000mm to 1800mm. In order to keep the aero balance of the R8 the same, Audi had modified the profile of the barge board element, and the radiator duct feed in the side pods.

At the start – indeed before the start – McNish and Davies were determined not only to stamp the R8's authority on the race early on, but also to lead themselves. As they exited the Ford chicane on their way to the start lane, the pair rubbed flanks and the radio airways turned blue. Davies, on the outside, won the contest and, for nine hours, the car that he shared with former Le Mans winners Johnny Herbert and Guy Smith, led the race.

The contest lost much of its potential following a pivotal incident just before 6.00pm. McNish was still in second place, just ahead of JJ Lehto in the Champion Audi, the Zytek challenge never having materialised. Both cars hit a patch of oil and water, laid down by the PK Sport Porsche

Allan McNish can no longer remember how he got his trashed car back to the pits. (Author's collection)

Champion entry leads that of Team Goh at the start of the 2004 Le Mans. The Veloqx cars have already gone past and look to be the favourites, but fortunes will change and it is the Goh car that will win. (Author's collection)

With McNish hors de combat, Biela and Kaffer did a stirling job, charging through the traffic to bring their delayed car home in fifth. (Author's collection)

GT3-RS on the Porsche Curves. Such was the force of McNish's impact against the barriers that Lehto afterwards told him the his eye were like clocks; "they were going round-and-round."

The Scot's car was badly damaged, and how he ever got it back to the pits is a piece of Le Mans folklore. With a front wheel awry and minus front bodywork, the car limped back, McNish on automatic pilot. Afterwards he could recall nothing of the incident from the time that he realised he was on oil and about to crash, to his waking up in hospital, "although I appeared perfectly compos mentis." As he got out of the car he collapsed, his subconscious realising that his duty had been done. The McNish was taken to hospital, his race over, the Audi UK mechanics went to work, and the car was rebuilt allowing Frank Biela and Pierre Kaffer not only to continue but to finish in an amazing fifth place, 29 laps behind the eventual winner.

"The R8 was so easy to repair," said Ulrich Baretzky. "Tell me another car that could have been repaired like McNish's in 2004." (The water temperature rose to 140 degrees as Allan returned to the pits.) "The engine started no trouble after that pit stop. It was bullet proof."

Meanwhile, up at the front Davies was forced to undergo a stop-go penalty for passing under yellow flags, and the Japanese R8, now in second place, unlapped itself. (Toward the start of the race this car had been suffering from a brake balance problem, causing Capello to end up in a gravel bed. It also caught fire after the Italian's final pit stop but, happily, this was extinguished immediately.) During the morning there followed what was the only lead change in the race – the Audi R8 years felt a bit like that. A seized rose-joint in the left-hand rear suspension forced Herbert to bring his British Audi into the pits, where it lost two laps. Davies now set off after the leader with a vengeance. The Englishman was, almost certainly, the star of that year's race; he certainly set the fastest lap, demonstrating an aggression that was perhaps missing during the rest of the season. Herbert, too, appeared determined, and in the

Late in the 2004 race, a pit stop for the Veloqx team. (Author's collection)

Time ticks away for Jamie Davies. Despite last minute heroics by team-mate Johnny Herbert, their car finished second only in 2004. (Author's collection)

run-up to the finish began to pull in the Goh Audi. The gap was down to 45 seconds with just an hour left. With the last pit stops over, it was down to 34 seconds. However, time was running out and an excursion across the gravel at the second Mulsanne chicane indicated to Herbert that he was not going to be able to catch the Japanese car. Team boss Kazumichi Goh was about to achieve his dream, and the

R8 to set a new distance record for Le Mans. It proved to be the closest finish at Le Mans since that classic Jacky Ickx (Ford) versus Hans Hermann (Porsche) battle of 1969.

Seiji Ara was in the Goh car for that final shift ensuring glory for Japan, but his co-drivers were that serial-Le Mans-winner Tom Kristensen and the latter's team-mate from the previous years Bentley win, Dindo Capello. When it

Emanuele Pirro (Italy)

Effervescent Emanuel Pirro was one of the trio that won three consecutive Le Mans for the R8. By 2007 the Roman had scored nine successive podium finishes at the race, including two more wins with the R10, while, as far as the R8 was concerned, he had taken 16 wins from 47 starts, and was also ALMS champion in 2005. The Italian raced in Formula 1, first with Benetton in 1989, and then with BMS Dallara. However, he was to state how much more enjoyable sports car racing was. Pirro left the Audi squad at the end of 2008 to make way for younger drivers. However, he had not finished with Le Mans and in 2010 he returned to the 24 hour race in Drayson Racing's Lola.

came to 1000km races, Team Goh seemed to be missing something, but at Le Mans it was a worthy winner. Perhaps that something was the Dane. It was also fitting that Capello, who had been so much involved in the history of the car, should have at last won Le Mans in an R8.

"I did not love the R8 until 2004," he remembered. "All the rest was perfect except every time we went to Le Mans. I won at Sebring, at Petit Le Mans and many other races in the American Le Mans Series. I achieved three pole positions at Le Mans, but did not seem to be able to win the race with the R8. Every time we were the quickest we had some problem that cut our chance of victory. When I won in 2003 with the Bentley on one side I was so happy. Until you actually win Le Mans you start to think that you will never do it. If you have a winning car and yet never win yourself then you start to think there is something wrong

with your luck. Once you win you lose a lot of the tension.

"The sad side of the first victory was that I hadn't done it with Audi, and I still did not know whether I would do it with Audi. Fortunately I had to wait just 12 months and the moment came. From that moment I started to like the R8 even more than before. People had always associated me with Audi but the first time I went in another car I showed that I could win, so the Bentley was the car I liked the most. However, my heart was quite sad because my heart was, and still is, with Audi."

Champions in America and Europe

Dave Maraj's operation returned to North America, while the other two teams remained in Europe to contest the Nürburgring 1000km, another classic race, even if the circuit could not be said to share the charisma of its predecessor. The adjacent location of the old and new Nürburgrings meant that there are some things that did not change – and one of these was the vagaries of the weather in the Eifel Mountains. Fitting the correct rubber became crucial during the race, as the conditions alternated between sunshine and rain. Kaffer aquaplaned into a gravel trap, sustained a slow puncture, and lost almost a lap, falling back to fifth place. The history of the Audi R8 is punctuated by stories of troubled cars fighting their way back up the field, and this was one of them as Kaffer and McNish clawed their way back ahead of the fellow UK R8, driven by Davies and Herbert, and to an eventual victory margin of one lap. The Goh R8 of Ara and Capello was back in fourth following an altercation with a GT car towards the end of the race.

Just over a month later, the three Audis were at Silverstone, recording a one-two-three, with the Japanese car in the middle this time. Kaffer and McNish scored a second consecutive victory with a fuel saving strategy that meant one less pit stop than their rivals. The Zytek had again proved a nuisance in practice. The enthusiastic Robbie Kerr was over 1.5 seconds faster than the Audi drivers, who were palpably trying hard. Even at the end of the first lap Kerr was disappearing into the distance. He lost the lead to the Audis during the first pit stops, but regained it with an enthusiastic demonstration of how to use back markers to great effect. A collision put the Zytek back in the pits and it eventually finished fourth. In the weeks that followed, the Zytek people modestly said that they probably could not have won anyway but their team, with a fraction of Audi's budget, had proved that, at last, the German cars could be challenged. You had to go back to 1999 to find a time when anything outside the Volkswagen Group could have done that.

The final round of the LMES was at Spa; the circuits certainly meant something that inaugural year. Here it was the turn of Davies and Herbert to win by a lap, the 50th victory for the R8 in just 60 starts. Ara and Capello were a lap behind in second place. However, there was disappointment for the Kaffer/McNish pairing, pre-race

favourites to clinch the LMES drivers' title. On just lap 23, the aggressive Kaffer collided with a GT Ferrari at the fast Blanchimont left-hander, and then slammed into a TVR; the Audi R8 caught fire leaving Davies and Herbert to score enough points to secure the championship. A minor misjudgment had decided the destination of the trophy. The Audi drivers dominated the final table, the two Englishmen scoring 34 points, six ahead of their Veloqx teams mates and seven ahead of the Goh drivers.

Over in North America, dear old R-505 was busy winning four out of the six remaining ALMS races, driven by JJ Lehto and Marco Werner. The Finnish/German duo fought the MG Lola of Chris Dyson and Andy Wallace at Mid-Ohio, before a spin lost the Dyson-entered car a lap. At Lime Rock it was Dyson's other MG Lola, driven by James Weaver and Butch Leitzinger, that finished second, this time under 1.5 seconds adrift. Most of the teams had changed tyres shortly after the start because of a rain shower. The R8 stayed on slicks, the track dried rapidly, and although an unluckily-timed first pit stop plus a stop-and-go penalty caused a wobble, it was still able to hold on to victory.

And so it continued. Sears Point was won by over a lap, once Werner had seen off the quicker of Dyson's two cars. A fourth consecutive victory, the first in ALMS history, came at Portland. This time Lehto and Werner had to work hard for their 1.09 second win, following a stop-and-go penalty for the Finn. His escapades that day have been described as legendary. Again it was a Dyson car that kept the Audi pair honest and, at Mosport, the American team with its British-built car received the rewards of its endeavours. Towards the end of the race the Audi suffered a puncture and Lehto slid in a tyre barrier losing almost a minute. The Leitzinger/Weaver swept by for an eventual 16 second win.

At Road America, Road Atlanta, and Laguna Seca it was back to business as usual. The first of these saw a collision at the start drop the Champion R8 back to ninth, but the car ran like clockwork, the Dyson team ran into trouble, and Lehto and Werner were rewarded by yet another one lap winning margin. At Petit Le Mans, Champion Racing entered two R8s for the first time, Lehto and Werner's

Team Veloqx returned to its winning ways at Silverstone, although the Davies/Herbert car seen here could finish in third place only. (Author's collection)

R8-505 being joined by LMES refugees Herbert and Kaffer in R8-605. As at Spa, the German collided with a GT – exactly the same Cirtek-entered Ferrari – and spent time in the gravel, leaving the season's regular R8 pairing to score a three lap victory. There had been some question as to whether fault lay with him or the Ferrari's driver Andrew Kirkaldy. At Road Atlanta, television coverage indicated that the guesting Kaffer was to blame. The nearest non-Audi, one of the Dyson MG Lolas, was 11 laps back in third place. The positions were reversed for the final ALMS round which took place at Laguna Seca, but the result was still a second one-two for the Champion team. Lehto and Werner suffered from two full-course yellows, leaving Herbert and Kaffer to win following a sudden cloudburst and a sprint to

Laguna Seca was the final race of 2004, with Pierre Kaffer and Johnny Herbert finishing in what looks, here, to be a spectacular first place. (Courtesy Gary Horrocks)

the chequered flag. Nevertheless, R-505's two drivers had finished the season ALMS champions, numerous points ahead of the Dyson quartet.

The year had shown that the R8 could still continue to win despite the withdrawal of the factory team. McNish pointed out that there was no difference between driving for the works and private teams. "[Joest technical director] Ralf Jüttner was at a lot of races while Dr Ullrich and his engineers walked between the teams." Re-engineering the R8 did not work, and when any of the private teams tried to do so, they found themselves returning to the original setups. It was as if, said McNish, Audi had handed them a car manual. "The back-up that David [Ingram] had instigated with Sam Li meant that the name of their team may have been Veloqx but it was easy for me to slip back into."

2005 – Audi R8
The days of the kingdom are numbered

Arguably, the Audi R8 was less active in its final full year, with just one car contesting the LMES. However, Champion was back up to two for all of the ALMS rounds and there were still three at Le Mans for the R8's swansong there, although, for the first time since 1999, Volkswagen Group cars were not the favourites to win the 24 hour race.

"With the restrictions on the car for 2005 and 2006 Audi had got the car to such a point that anybody could

Audi R8 at rest: Sebring 2005. (Courtesy Martin Spetz)

Allan McNish was teamed with Frank Biela and Emanuele Pirro for the 2005 Sebring 12 Hours. (Martin Spetz)

drive it fast," said Allan McNish. "Its calling card at the end of its life was that it was fast in the dry and the wet, the cold and the heat, at Lime Rock or Sears Point or Le Mans. It did not matter what condition you put it in; you knew that the R8 was secure underneath you."

It was the usual story at Sebring for the R8's final race there. In this case both Audis entered were run by Champion Racing. The pair swapped the lead with the quickest of the Dyson Lolas. However, reliability was a serious issue for all but the two German cars, and at

Guy Smith (England)
Guy Smith won at Le Mans, but not with an Audi, having been one of the Bentley squad in 2003. However, he had four races with an R8, twice for Stefan Johansson's Gulf team and twice for Team Veloqx. His only Le Mans with Audi was with the UK car in 2004, when he was part of the second place team. Although still based in Yorkshire, Smith became a regular driver for the Dyson team in the ALMS. With Dyson confined to North America, he also continued to appear at Le Mans, driving an LMP2 Lola and then a Zytek for the Quifel-ASM team in 2008 and 2009, and then an LMP1 Rebellion Lola for the following year two years.

the finish they were 6.365 seconds apart, the closest competitive finish – yes, the team-mates were still racing – at Sebring, but a massive 20 laps ahead of the third placed car. At last, Champion Racing had won the 12-hour race after a succession of near misses, although it was, ironically, second yet again as well. For the record, it was R-605 driven by Tom Kristensen, JJ Lehto, and Marco Werner that came first, in front of Frank Biela, Allan McNish, and Emanuele Pirro in R8-505. There had been little in it between the two crews, and the outcome was probably decided in the pits. With just over an hour to go, Werner had a 12 second lead when he came into the pits to hand over to Kristensen for the penultimate pit stop. The chasing McNish also pitted, but was staying in his car and taking on fuel only while the Dane was being given new tyres. In theory, the lead should have changed at this point. What happened next was probably the key to the whole race. Kristensen, realising that he needed to get out ahead of McNish, decided that he might be able to get away with less fuel than originally planned, particularly as there was still one more pit stop to go. This saved between seven and nine seconds. McNish was slightly impeded by a television camera crew and Kristensen left the pit lane still a couple of seconds ahead. Although now on cold tyres, he pushed hard to ensure he kept that lead, and was able to give himself an 11 second advantage that doubled when McNish himself took on a fresh set of Michelins during his final stop. Initially the fresh rubber meant that Allan could claw back something of that lead, but once they had lost their edge the race was effectively over.

The old one-two: Audi again dominated Sebring in 2005. (Courtesy Martin Spetz)

"That fight Tom and I had at Sebring in 2005 was titanic," remembered McNish. "If it had been against another type of car everybody would have been jumping up and down. Because it was against a sister car people thought it was staged managed, but I can tell you we were going for it. It was Brad [Kettler], the sod – I couldn't believe when he short filled Tom's car. Afterwards Tom and I said that it would be easier for us to drive together. We were every man for himself. All Dr Ullrich says is 'boys, don't crash into each other.' He has the trust in us to know what we're doing but he also knows that we're racing drivers and probably would not listen anyway. It's a fine line."

Unlike previous years, there was more ALMS activity before Le Mans. The Dyson team was again the threat at Road Atlanta, where Lehto and Werner went into the lead with only 30 minutes to go following a stop-and-go-penalty, imposed, it was said, because a wheel developed a mind of its own. Biela and Pirro had a damaged wheel that lost

Thanks to the modular design of the R8, Lehto's car was repaired following a collision with a GT car during the early laps, and Werner was able to take it to 18th place at Mid-Ohio. (Courtesy Martin Spetz)

Never give up: Marco Werner continues on at Mid-Ohio. (Courtesy Martin Spetz)

them a couple of laps, and they finished in third. Another stop-and-go, this time for Biela and Pirro, meant that the best they could do at an action–filled Mid-Ohio was to finish third behind the Dyson cars. Lehto, unfortunately, collected a spinning GT 2 car that he encountered as he crested the rise at Turn 11. It was 40 minutes before Werner could take the repaired car back out onto the track and claim an eventual 18th place. Third for the leading Audi doesn't sound too good, but Champion Racing was now on its way to Le Mans, and its finest hour.

While the Audi R8s remained favourites to win in the ALMS, the situation was different in Europe. The ACO rule changes, which meant the R8s had to start with 50 kilograms of additional ballast and 30hp less power, levelled the playing field here and the Pescarolos and Zyteks became a real threat. Indeed, the French built cars were regarded as the favourites for that year's Le Mans, and it was expected that Henri Pescarolo would follow up his four overall wins there as a driver with one as a constructor. However, two months before Le Mans there was the matter of an LMES

An unsual state of affairs: the highest placed Audi, that of Biela and Pirro, comes third at Mid-Ohio. (Courtesy Martin Spetz)

round at Spa-Francorchamps and here, despite being competitive, neither Audi nor Pescarolo was to win.

A sole Audi R8 had been entered for the 2005 LMES. Run by Hughes de Chaunac's ORECA team, and driven at the opening round by Frenchman Jean-Marc Gounon and Monaco's Stéphane Ortelli, it seemed Gallic enough. However, the car was, in fact, that owned by Audi UK and, for the last three races of the season, Ortelli was joined by Scot Allan McNish. The presence of Wolfgang Ullrich at every round indicated that the factory was keeping its

eye on the car. (Audi UK still owns the now rebuilt car, occasionally displaying it at West London Audi. It also retains one of the R8Cs from 1999, the other now being at Ingolstadt. As an example of how they are now used, in 2010 R8 and R8C were both seen on display at Audi UK's 'Power Collection' press driving event. "We have no intention of ever disposing of it!" exclaimed Ingram, of R8-603.)

The Spa race was held in a typical Ardennes mist. A Pescarolo took the pole and a Zytek won, but the

The ORECA R8 emerges from the mist at Spa. (Author's collection)

ORECA Audi was involved in the battle for the lead almost throughout. By the end of the fourth hour, things were looking good for ORECA as the car required only one more pit stop, as opposed to the two each of its rivals. However, in the last hour Gounon spun off at the 'Bus Stop' chicane. Although the Frenchman made it back to the pits, front suspension damage meant that the car had to retire, leaving

the factory Zytek of Hayanari Shimoda, John Neilsen, and Caspar Elgaard to come home first.

Le Mans

As Dr Ullrich was to point out, Le Mans is different each season. "It offers a new and unpredictable challenge every year." For the first time since the dawn of the new

Having driven an R8 at Le Mans in 2000, Stéphane Ortelli, seen here going through Spa's fearsome Eau Rouge bend, was back behind the wheel of one for 2005. (Author's collection)

millennium, a Volkswagen Group car was not the favourite to win the 2005 running of the race. The regulation changes had made the R8 approximately five seconds per lap slower than its main competitors. The money was on France's Henri Pescarolo (the factory Zytek had, strangely, been refused an entry) to follow in the footsteps of fellow countryman Jean Rondeau as a winning driver/constructor even if he had now long retired from being behind the wheel. The early laps suggested that this would be so as his two cars streaked off into the lead. A Dome had also got ahead of the Audis.

Brad Kettler recalls that the two Champion entries had been "quite slow" in practice. "We knew that we were not

The leaders are well on their way, as the ORECA Audi R8 heads the rest of the pack at the start of Le Mans 2005.
(Author's collection)

Champion leads ORECA through the Esses at Le Mans. (Author's collection)

going to outrun anybody on outright speed so we were looking for balance, consistency and so forth. It was morning warm up and JJ (Lehto) was scheduled to drive the whole thing." The television cameras were following the car around the circuit. "There was the long telephoto shot, taken from the first Mulsanne chicane looking up towards Tertre Rouge, past the linden trees. JJ came over the radio – and he never did this kind of thing very often, platitudes were not part of his persona – and said 'guys, the car is absolutely perfect, it's as good as it's going to be'." As if on cue, the car came into view on the monitors, looking as if it was almost floating. It was an enormous morale booster to his crew; Kettler, who was out on the pit wall by himself recalled that it gave him "goose bumps." He went back onto the crew-only radio channel so that Lehto could not hear him and told them he had a plan, which was simply to now wipe off the car, wax it, push it outside, and put a cover on it.

At the end of the first hour of the race, two of three R8s were holding an unaccustomed third and fourth place behind the Pescarolos, the quickest of Champion's pair ahead of the ORECA car. (The US and French teams were running radically different settings, Champion having opted for high downforce and, thus, better cornering speed, while ORECA was trying for as high a straight line speed as possible.) The Dome had already lost time in the pits and the Pescarolos were now in the Audis' firing line. The French cars were refuelling every 12 laps compared to the 13 of the R8s, thanks to the latter's direct injection. Then one of them collided with a GT and dropped back to seventh. One down, so to speak. Then, the lead car came into the pits with gear change problems. It fell even further back than its stable mate. Two down, and with less than three hours to go, and the R8 was back in its accustomed spot – first – the Pirro/McNish/Biela Champion car heading the field.

There are places at Le Mans that permit a commanding view of an Audi. (Author's collection)

That lead disappeared during the evening, as a tired Emanuele Pirro, triple stinting, probably lost concentration behind the safety car and went straight on into the tyres at Arnage. Into the lead went the Champion's other entry, driven up to this point by JJ Lehto and Marco Werner, and the slowest Audi in practice, with Rollcentre's Dallara second, ahead of the ORECA R8, and then the erstwhile leader. At 8.45pm, into the lead car went one Tom Kristensen for the first time in the race. The Dane was now on his way to a remarkable sixth successive win at Le Mans

By half distance the Champion Audis occupied the first two places, with the ORECA car, which had been troubled by a broken wishbone, back in fifth. However, as the following day dawned, McNish went off into the gravel trap at Indianapolis, a subsequent 20 minute pit stop for suspension repair dropping his car back from second to third, four laps behind the leaders. Shortly before, Kristensen had nearly collected the errant ORECA R8 in the Ford chicane.

The race now ran its course, although Kristensen did later take a trip through one of the gravel traps – his car showing the dirt as only a white car can after 17 hours at Le Mans. By contrast, the other Champion R8, its nose changed after its earlier excursion, appeared pristine. With about an hour and a half to go, Pescarolo decided to be content with second place as his remaining car's engine began to overheat. No longer under any pressure, Kristensen was able to ease off. Once favourite, now underdog, the Audi R8 could win at Le Mans whatever its status.

Kristensen had added his own remarkable record to the Audi R8's list of achievements. "I happen to have been one of the drivers for all the R8's victories at Le Mans," said Kristensen, on being asked what the car meant to him. "I also won the car's first race at Sebring. It has had an

The third place Audi heads under the Dunlop Bridge. R8s were always shod on Michelin tyres. (Author's collection)

Final victory salute for the R8 at Le Mans. (Author's collection)

enormous meaning for my career. It was why I immediately ordered a road car when one was named after the R8!"

After the first R8 Le Mans victory, Tony Southgate had pointed out that one win would not be enough. "The worst thing Audi could have done on winning Le Mans in 2000 would have been to simply put the trophy in a cupboard and gloat as BMW had done the year before. If your car is winning," Southgate told Audi, "hone it and keep racing at Le Mans until it becomes obsolete. Then you will become a Le Mans 'name'." Now, Southgate said: "I am pleased to see that is what they have done. Audi is down there with all the historic names of Le Mans."

The race had certainly changed the public perception of Audi. It was not just that it was, as Dr Ullrich pointed out, "one of the three races worldwide that are known to people who are not even interested in motor racing." There was also the fact that, as he added, "the Le Mans rule book gives you the chance to race with the technology that fits your brand strategy."

The R8 was now, undoubtedly, dated, even if it had just won again. "The results we had from 2000 to 2006 speak for themselves, stated Capello. "We won everything. We still improved the car a little bit each year but the base stayed the same. It is surely uncommon for a car to win for five years in a row without a major change. When the new generation of sports cars, which were quicker, started arriving then the reliability of the R8 and the professionalism of the team made the difference."

To say that winning Le Mans is a tiring business, in 2005 as much as any other year, would be to state the obvious. (Courtesy Tim Wagstaff)

The R8 feels its age

The ORECA Audi missed Monza but was out again for the 1000km of Silverstone, the weather conditions at which made the Spa contest seem positively congenial. A local team, Creation, with its DBA-Judd, dominated most of the race, having started from pole. The 4.00pm start was in drizzle that, by the end of the first hour, had become heavy rain. McNish pursued the DBA in the R8, but lost a lap following a fuel stop under safety car conditions. At the start of the fifth hour, and now racing in the dark, Jamie Campbell-Walter in the DBA still had a 54 second lead over the Scot, but it was a lead that was being eroded. Yet another safety car period reduced the lead to a few seconds, and at 9.21pm the Audi moved into first place. When it came to such a fight, the tenacious McNish was possibly the best person to have in an R8. A final pit stop and driver change to Ortelli saw what had been a widening gap cut back to six seconds – but, out of the blue, Ortelli set the fastest lap of the race to secure victory.

It was to be the only one for the Audi in that year's LMS. At both the Nürburgring and in Istanbul, the car finished in second place. In Germany, McNish had been in the lead during the final hour, but an inspired Hayanari Shimoda, who had been forced to start from the back of the grid due to an irregularity with his Zytek's airbox, forced his way past with about 10 minutes remaining. In Turkey the R8 was again in the fight for the lead toward the end, but this time it was in the fifth hour and by the works Pescarolo that it was relegated to second place. Audi Playstation Team ORECA took third place in the LMES LMP1 team championship, McNish and Ortelli finishing in the same spot on the LMP1 drivers' table. These were the only championships the Audi R8 ever lost.

Over in North America, the two Champion Audis were having a busy time completing the season, usually fighting with the Dyson Lolas. At Lime Rock they saw off Leitzinger and Weaver, pulling away when the latter's car failed to

Grim weather conditions at Silverstone in 2005 provided Allan McNish with the opportunity for another spectacular drive to victory. (Courtesy Tim Wagstaff)

fire up immediately after its final pit stop. Leitzinger had, though, harried the Audis in the early stages and at one point the Lola had led the race. Lehto and Werner won the internal scrap between the Audis by a mere 1.719 seconds. Contact with a Porsche seemed to have damaged the other car's chances, but Pirro had fought back, trying to pass Lehto in Turn 1 during a re-start after a full-course yellow, but was foiled by Lehto's outbraking manoeuvre. Biela and Pirro then took their first win of the season by finishing first at Sears Point, benefiting from an argument that Werner had with a GT car, a collision that resulted in the change of the right-hand upper wishbone.

The pattern of the season now changed in favour of R8-505's drivers, as far as the Champion team was concerned. At Portland it won despite a 20 second penalty, although they only took the lead on the penultimate lap when Weaver ran out of fuel. Lehto crashed spectacularly when the entire wing of his car flew off. Lehto and Werner led for many laps at Road America, before a stop-and-go dropped them back to an eventual third, leaving Pirro and Biela to win again, the two Audis split, perhaps not surprisingly, by a Dyson Lola. At Mosport, Lehto and Werner fought hard with Leitzinger and Weaver, the lead changing hands five times before the Dyson car won. Biela and Pirro finished a lap back, but were convincing 12 lap winners a month later at Petit Le Mans, taking the drivers' title. Lehto was involved in a start line collision, attempting to overtake pole sitter Hayanari Shimoda's Zytek, with James Weaver trying to make it a threesome into Turn 1. However, he and Werner were able to carve their way back to seventh overall. It was the R8's sixth consecutive PLM victory.

Audi had twice lost to the lighter Zytek in Europe, and for the final two North American races of the season it was again faced by the Repton factory's car, driven by Shimoda and Tom Chilton. The Japanese driver served notice of intent by claiming pole position for Petit Le Mans, and the pair then won at Laguna Seca in what was, arguably, the most exciting race of the ALMS season. Biela and Pirro finished second, the Italian having managed his fuel better towards the end than Lehto, who dropped back to fourth as a result. That meant he and Werner could only manage fourth place in the championship, Chris Dyson splitting the Audi teams. At Laguna Seca the lead had changed many times between five of the LMP category cars, with an LMP2 newcomer, a Porsche Spyder, staying close. *Mene, Mene, Tekel, Upharsin*. The writing was on the wall; the days of the R8's kingdom were now numbered.

Contrasting fortunes. The number one car, seen here driven by Werner, failed to finish at Portland in 2005, after team-mate Lehto had spun the car spectacularly following a collision in which their car's rear bodywork mounting had been damaged. Biela (seen following) and Pirro won the race. (Courtesy Gary Horrocks)

Audi R8 2005 Le Mans specification

Vehicle type: Le Mans Prototype (LMP1)
Chassis: Carbon fibre monocoque, crash structure ACO and FIA approved, CFK rollbars front and rear, carbon fibre body
Engine: V8, turbo charged, 90-degree cylinder angle, 4 valves per cylinder, 2 Garrett turbo chargers, to comply with the rules 2x29.9mm air restrictors and boost pressure restriction to 1.67bar absolute, direct fuel injection FSI
Engine management: Bosch MS 2.9
Engine lubrication: Dry sump, Shell lubricants
Displacement: 3600cc
Output (approx): 520hp
Torque: >700Nm
Transmission: Rear-wheel drive
Clutch: CFK clutch
Gearbox: Sequential 6-speed sports gearbox, partner Ricardo
Differential: Multiple-disc limited-slip differential
Driveshafts: Constant-velocity plunging tripod joints
Steering: Rack-and-pinion power steering
Suspension: Independent suspension front and rear, double-wishbone suspension, pushrod system with spring/damper unit, adjustable gas-filled shock absorbers
Brakes: Hydraulic dual-circuit brake system, monobloc light-alloy brake calipers, ventilated carbon fibre discs front and rear, driver-adjustable brake balance
Rims: OZ forged magnesium rims, Front: 13.5x18in, Rear: 14.5x18in
Tyres: Michelin Radial, Front: 33/65-18, Rear: 37/71-18
Length: 4650cm
Width: 2000cm
Height: 1080cm
Minimum weight: 950kg
Fuel tank capacity: 80 litres

Andy Wallace (England)

When it came to the great long distance races of the late 1980s and the 1990s, Oxford-born Andy Wallace was one of the most successful competitors. Having won at Le Mans for Jaguar in 1988, early in his career, the former F3000 driver British Formula 3 champion went on to come first in the 24 Hours of Daytona three times, win the Sebring 12 Hours twice, and the Petit Le Mans once. He had eight drives in a Champion R8, contesting the 2001 ALMS season and the 2002 Sebring with the team. In 2006, the peripatetic Wallace was to add to his overall victory at Le Mans, when he shared the LMP2 class-winning RML Lola. He became the only person to have competed with an R8 in both contemporary and 'historic' racing, when he drove Jim Rogers' cars.

NB: The R8's technical specifications altered from 2000 to 2006, with the move to the TFSi engine in 2001, and increasingly stringent regulations that saw the claimed output fall from 610bhp to 520bhp, and the fuel tank capacity reduced from 90 to 80 litres.

2006 – Audi R8
Occasional appearances

The Audi factory sports car team returned to the tracks for the 2006 Sebring and, of course, won again (Audi was to come first at Sebring on eight consecutive occasions, between 2000 and 2007). However, this was not another victory for the R8. The diesel era had arrived and the TDI-engined R10 was now Audi's weapon of choice. Having race tested the R10 in Florida, Audi then took to honing the car away from the public gaze and kept its ALMS hand in by allowing Champion to bring R8-605 out for three final flings.

At Houston's Reliant Park, Dindo Capello and Allan McNish dominated the results, the R8 being the only prototype to complete the 2hr 45 min race. The second place car, a GT Corvette, was five laps back. However, LMP2 Porsche Spyders were now a fact of life, and 160 kilograms lighter than the R8. New regulations had meant that the R8 now weighed 935kg, and in qualifying for the Houston race the Audi had been only fourth fastest, beaten by a Dyson Lola and two of the Porsches. The race began in the evening, and as dusk had changed to darkness, so Capello had moved up to second. Pit stop strategy then took McNish into the lead. The Porsches fell by the wayside, but it should be pointed out that Dindo recorded the fastest lap. Considering the fact that the bumpy and slippery Houston circuit was hardly ideal for a car designed to win at Le Mans, the R8 was still putting in impressive performances. The car could run at a race pace closer to its qualifying times than its rivals.

The start of the farewell tour. Allan McNish's Audi R8 under the lights at Houston, in 2006. (Courtesy Joe Martin)

At a resurfaced Mid-Ohio the two Penske-entered Porsches pushed the Champion Audi, which was also troubled by one of its old advisories from the Dyson team, back to third. Dave Maraj had reckoned that McNish had done an "outstanding" job to qualify in second place with his five-year old car, but Dr Ullrich said that it was becoming increasingly impossible to compete with the lighter LMP2 projectiles. Both drivers struggled to get sufficient temperature in their tyres during the race. The only consolation, a scant one, was that they at least won the LMP1 class yet again.

McNish brakes on his way to victory at Houston. (Courtesy Martin Spetz)

The Audi could do no better than third behind the LMP2 Porsche Spyders at Mid-Ohio. (Courtesy Martin Spetz)

Lime Rock on July 1 was the true swan song of the R8. The two LMP2 Porsches made sure that it was not going to be easy, and it was not until the start of the second hour that McNish moved to the front, the Champion car having performed poorly during qualifying. One hour before the finish, a safety car period caused the Scot to lose the lead but, in typical McNish fashion, he mounted a counter attack and 30 minutes later regained first place. It was a victory that gave McNish, whose first R8 win had come at this same New England track back in 2000, and Capello particular pleasure, and a fitting end to the career of one of sports car racing's all-time most successful contestants. "My other car is a diesel," proclaimed a sticker on Lime Rock-winning R8-605.

Despite his time away in Formula 1, with Toyota, Allan McNish was among the fastest R8 pilots, and it was fitting that he should have been one of the two drivers for the farewell tour. (Courtesy Martin Spetz)

Dindo Capello partnered McNish during that final season. (Courtesy Martin Spetz)

"The last victory was quite an emotional moment for Dindo and I," said McNish. "We were not very quick in qualifying. In the race we had the normal situation, a horrible, bumpy undulating track with lots of traffic and we won. The R8 did its job again.

"There was a question as to whether there would be something different for the livery for this final send off, but it was very subtle, with the names of all the drivers that had won in an R8 on the bodywork. The car made a lot of drivers' careers.

Over the hill? Not quite; the Audi R8 won two out of its three races in 2006. (Courtesy Martin Spetz)

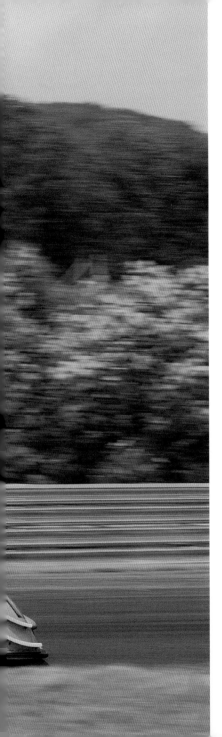

The final triumph at Lime Rock. (Courtesy Joe Martin)

"I don't think that, because of the evolution of cars and competition, such a car will ever happen again," added McNish. "Ask most drivers about their cars and they will refer to them as 'it' but R8 drivers talk about 'she'. 'She' got under my skin a little bit. 'She' saved my life. 'She' gave me that first Audi title in Adelaide, the chance to carve out my name as it is now in sports car racing, and taught me a lot about development. You could have pretty heroic drives in that car. 'She' also identified me with the Audi brand. There will never be another R8.

"The R8 was the perfect handling car. It was reactive and easily adjustable," reflected Ulrich Baretzky. "Every driver is still dreaming of it."

Audi was to win the three consecutive Le Mans following the retirement of the R8, but it was never the same again. The advent of the diesel era first brought out Peugeot, with an announcement that it would enter such a car. Audi, however, stole a march and its new R10 was the only diesel on the grid for 2006. The following year, a Peugeot 908 HDi FAP actually led, even if it was only as far as the first bend on the opening lap. By 2008 the French cars were the favourites and it was only Audi's vast Le Mans experience, and the tenacity of its driver line-up – Kristensen, Capello and McNish – that gave the Volkswagen

A brave new world awaits. (Courtesy Joe Martin)

A new sight on the Mulsanne Straight for 2006. That year, the R8 was replaced by the first of the diesels, the Audi R10. This and its successors, the R15 plus and the R18, were also to win at Le Mans. (Author's collection)

Group its ninth consecutive Le Mans. For the first time in the 21st century it knew that it had been in a real fight.

To counter the French menace, Audi brought out the R15, while the R10 continued in private hands. Although it enjoyed a hat-trick of Le Mans wins, the R10 never matched the R8's history. Goaded by the R15's defeat in 2009, Audi developed the aerodynamically more efficient R15 plus for the following year, but the Peugeots were still faster.

Despite this, Audi still scored a one-two-three in the 24 hour race. All four 908s retired, most with engine failure; a classic hare and tortoise story. In recent years the diesel Audis have faced a challenger such as the R8 never saw, but the 2010 Le Mans underlined the fact that the company has proved its ability to build cars that beat not just the opposition but, and this is surely a greater accolade, the very nature of endurance races.

The diesel era meant that the Volkswagen Group had a strong rival in LMP1, for the first time since 2000. (Author's collection)

Marco Werner (Germany)

A former Daytona 24 Hours and Monaco Formula 3 winner, Dortmund's Marco Werner had been racing in the Porsche Supercup when he joined Audi in 2002. Despite this huge leap, he twice took the American Le Mans Series title, first with Joest in 2003, and then with Champion the following year. It was with the American team that he won his first Le Mans, in 2005 – the only time he was to do so in an R8. However, two more consecutive Le Mans victories followed with the diesel R10. His final Le Mans with Audi was in 2009, and the following year he signed with Highcroft to race its LMP2 HPD at La Sarthe. With 14 victories from 32 starts, he had been another of the R8's multi-winners.

Audi Powers Lola

During 2007, the Audi R8's engine made a surprise return to Le Mans and the Le Mans Series. In the April of that year, while the press was attending a preview of the Silverstone Classic festival, a Lola B07/10 was on the Northamptonshire track's South Circuit, testing for the first time with a V8 FSi engine identical to that used to win the 2005 Le Mans. The entrant for the car was the Swiss Spirit team whose principal, Fred Stadler, had, thanks to his connections with the Volkswagen Group and, in particular, engineer Heinz Lehmann, been able to convince Audi that such a project was feasible.

The FSi engine had little in common with the Judd engine more likely to be fitted to such a car, but the entire project was completed in 11 weeks, from start to finish. Key elements of the installation package included custom cast aluminium bell housing with integral oil tank; specially built monocoque with custom engine mounts; bespoke carbon composite air intake assembly, and Megaline semi-automatic gearshift system. A debut third place for the Lola-Audi at Valencia in the May proved it could work.

At Le Mans the patriotically red and white liveried Swiss car was driven by Iraj Alexander, Jean-Denis Deletraz – who had put the project together – and Marcel Fassler. Following an off-day before, the car qualified 14th on the grid, but then ran as high as seventh at the end of the first hour, before dropping back after a whole series of troubles, and eventually retiring with electrical issues just before midnight. After Le Mans, budgetary problems intervened and the project disappeared from sight.

Swiss Spirit's Audi FSi-engined Lola was first seen testing at Silverstone. Lola designer, Julian Soul (far right), was on hand. (Author's collection)

Rain was a feature of Le Mans in 2007. The Lola-Audi first stopped on the track at about 4.30pm, spun after colliding with a Panoz two hours later, and then, just after 7.00pm, stopped again. It eventually crawled back to the pits to have its electric harness checked, but was retired shortly before midnight. (Author's collection)

2007 onwards – Audi R8
Clone wars

Audi headquarters at Ingolstadt, Germany, may once have been the world centre for the Audi R8, but no longer. About 100 miles east of Indianapolis – home of the famed 500 mile race – out on the Indiana/Ohio border, is the small town of West College Corner. This is the home of Kettler Motor Werks, run by former Champion Racing chief engineer Brad Kettler. The perhaps remote location is for no other reason than that Kettler was brought up here, the son of an academic from the local university, situated just over the state line in the appropriately named town of Oxford. It is doubtful that anyone outside of the Audi factory knows more about the R8 than the affable American.

Here at West College Corner, you are likely to find R8-605, last of the official Audi R8s to be built and winner not only of the 2005 Le Mans 24 Hours, but also the R8's 'last race,' resplendent in the one-off livery in which it ran that day in Lime Rock, and still owned by Audi Sport North America. (The car was last driven at a Kettler Motor Werks 'reunion' in 2008, by Canadian sports car veteran Bill Adam.) However, there is far more to the story.

Lime Rock 2006 may have been the last race

Bill Adam leads Aaron Hsu during the 2008 Walter Mitty meeting at Road Atlanta. (Courtesy Martin Spetz)

Brad Kettler feels admiration for the R8's Ricardo gearbox. (Author's collection)

for the Audi R8 as a current car. However, it lives on in 'historic' racing, if the word 'historic' can correctly be applied to such a recent piece of machinery. In fact, Jim Rogers, owner of a Florida-based citrus growing company, ensured it would be so used even before that final victory in Connecticut. Rogers acquired chassis R8-405, which Champion Racing had used for just the one season, 2001, and announced that he wanted to use it for historic racing. "It was a tough sell," recalled Kettler. "This was 2003 and the R8 was still active in modern competition." Still, Kettler and Rogers were able to convince organisers of the HSR (Historic Sports car Racing) and SVRA (Sports car Vintage Racing Association) series that it could race as a historic. Now they had to work on how they could be run privately.

On to the scene also came chassis R8-403. This had been the Gulf-liveried car of Phil Bennett, although nobody knew who had owned it at the time, the idea being for Stefan Johansson to give the car a race history. It was sold to Aaron Hsu, who had seen that Rogers had been able to run his car without a large staff. A couple more were also sold to the pair. Hsu additionally purchased the first Team Goh car, R8-501 (as well as a 2001 Bentley EXP Speed 8), while Rogers acquired chassis R8-607, a 'clone' car, of which more anon.

Kettler could see that there was a lot of business to be had in this style of racing. It was no longer just a matter of relatively basic cars, such as Chevrolet stock block engined Lola T70s.

R8-606 and R8-607 are what Kettler calls 'clones.' These aren not official Audi issued cars, but they are "100 per cent" accurate. They have become the most actively used R8s of today. The first was built by Champion Racing at the end of 2005, the second in 2009 by Brad, former Champion mechanic Bobby Green, Greg Martin, and Greg Laird at Kettler Motor Werks. Kettler states that Champion had been left with "a glut" of spares including a monocoque, and R8-607 was a way of making sure that they were not wasted. "The car was built with Audi's knowledge. They did not really approve of it but we did, at one stage, discuss having homologation papers for it." The disapproval cannot have been too great, for Kettler still works with the factory, having also been a significant race and test engineer for Ingolstadt with the R10, R15, and now with the R18.

Joe Graziano leads the field through Road Atlanta's sweeping bends, with Bill Adam further down the field. (Courtesy Martin Spetz)

The first clone, R8-606, is said to be an excellent car, having been built with the best of the spares left over from the factory-built cars. It was bought by Tom Gonzales. "He was the perfect purchaser at the time. We were not sure how the whole operation would go and if we would continue to get support from the factory once the R8s had been truly retired." Gonzales acquired the car with the idea that it would never be run, but would simply go into a museum in Reno, Nevada. It was there for several years before being purchased by Travis Engen, an extremely fit sixty-something aerospace engineer by training, and an enthusiastic supporter of historic racing.

Engen made contact with Kettler to see if he would run the car, and in 2010 drove over 6000 kilometres in it with zero technical trouble. "He drove the wheels off of it," says Kettler affectionately. Brad praises Engen's attitude in learning to drive a flat-bottom sports car, and the way in which he supports him in running the car. Parts are becoming rarer but Kettler Motor Werks has acquired the R8 spares inventory of not only Champion Racing, but also that held by the factory at Ingolstadt. The latter was brought to West College Corner during early 2010 and included "everything that [Audi] had left when the car was retired." The KMW stock now has two, complete spare direct injection engines and ten Megaline shift units. He is another to describe Megaline as having been a major contributor to the success of the R8.

Kettler's company can now manufacture carbon fibre replica body panels using factory drillings and drawings, while it also has a stock of old bodywork and wings that it is able to repair. It is an impressive operation being, as Kettler points out, "a small company with limited resources." It is understandably important to him that he has Audi's blessing. This stock of parts is solely for possible future use on Audi R8s, to extend their longevity – Kettler believes that the 2002 variant is the most sustainable – and will never be used for anything else. "We are keeping it all out of the trash can."

Like Engen, Jim Rogers is also active with one of his cars, R8-607; he did race his factory-built R8-405 when he

Everything you could ever need for an Audi R8 can be found at Kettler Motor Werks. (Author's collection)

first acquired it. Now it is the 'clone' that he takes to the racetracks, although it was thought at the end of 2010 that both would appear the following season. Confusingly, both of them are in Champion livery and numbered '38.' Rogers no longer drives the cars but hires professionals Andy Wallace and Bill Adam to race them. Butch Leitzinger also shared the driving of the 'clone' at Sebring, when Wallace was busy on Le Mans Series duties with the RML LMP2 Lola. The two R8s have created "a big umbrella" of work for Kettler Motor Werks. Towards the end of 2007, while Brad was still working for Champion, it was becoming obvious that there were problems with serviceability. A 'reunion' was therefore organised for the beginning of the next year to coincide with the testing of the R10 diesel. Kettler rented Sebring for a day as part of a three-day clinic. The cars then still racing, R8-403, R8-501, R8-605, and Hsu's Bentley, were brought together, examined, documented, serviced, and then rolled out.

In 2010 the most active cars still racing in the USA were the 'clones' R8-606 and R8-607. Joest-liveried R8-502 and the Bentley were, by then, owned by George Stauffer, having been traded for a Le Mans-winning Ford during that summer. At the end of 2010, R8-403 was the property of Joe Graziano and, although he had raced it, it was then residing in factory colours, in a hanger in Hamilton, Montana. Negotiations were, however, being conducted through Brad

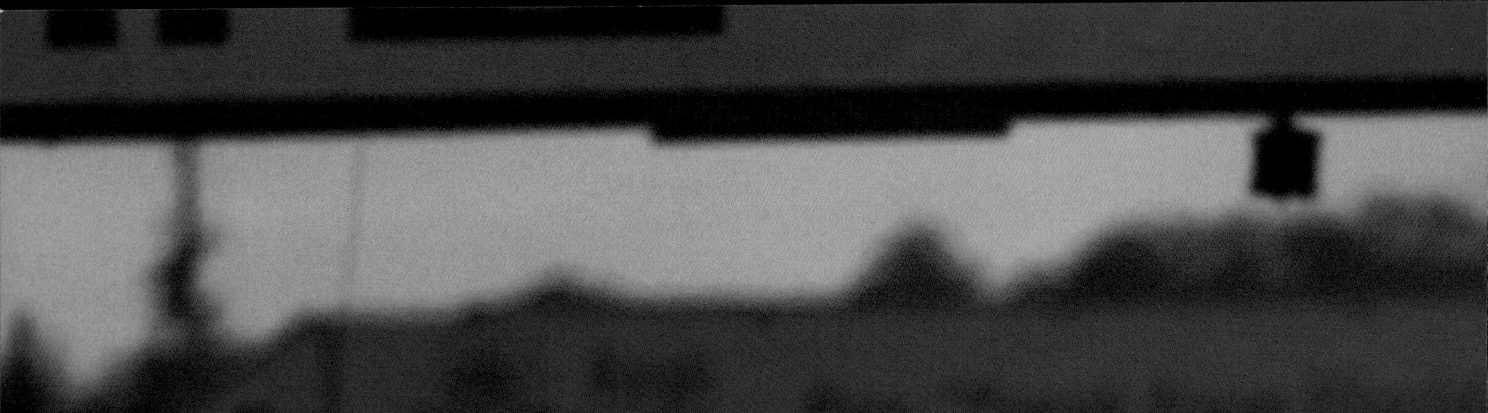

for this to return to Europe. Two years ago Adrian Hamilton, son of 1953 Le Mans winner Duncan Hamilton, started a project on behalf of an anonymous client – pseudonym 'Mr Rofgo' – to build a collection of cars that had raced in Gulf Oil colours. The ROFGO Collection, as it is known, commenced with a Ford GT40 and is now, as Adrian states, "16 cars and many millions of pounds later." The former Stefan Johansson car was purchased in 2011 from Graziano, and returned to Gulf livery for addition to the Hampshire, UK-based collection.

There are now around half a dozen opportunities for the R8s to race each year, at tracks such as Sebring, Road Atlanta, Elkhart Lake, and Watkins Glen, with main races that last from one to four hours and short sprints of just a few laps. Fields of over 60 have been known, with cars ranging from the Audis to elderly Corvettes. The organisers are, perhaps understandably, not massively strict on the regulations, which means that, say, a Riley & Scott that would never have beaten an Audi R8 during its heyday can now possibly do so thanks to modern modifications that mean it can have around 300bhp more power. Championships are based on class scores so, overall, signify little. However, Engen finished sixth in the SVRA's Mike Scott Enduro Series in 2010, despite competing in only four of the seven rounds.

Former Le Mans, Sebring, and Daytona winner, Andy Wallace, who prior to the R8s' resurrection had last driven one at Sebring in 2002, has been reminded why it was "one of the most perfect sports cars ever built. It was designed to be a very practical car. Everything works; you switch it on and there is never a hiccup. It is still the same today." Bobby Green, who was one of those who built Rogers' car and who now runs it, was Wallace's number one mechanic when he raced for Champion with Johnny Herbert in 2001. What is more, Wallace still uses the same R8 seat that was made for him back then.

What is arguably the most successful of all the R8s has also remained Stateside, although it is no longer raced. R8-505, described by Kettler, who engineered most of its many wins, as a "phenomenal race car" was sold by Champion in 2006 in a totally race-ready state, and is now in the possession of RM Motorsports of Wixom, Michigan. "It has not been started since the day we bought it," said RM owner Bud Bennett, although it has occasionally been put on display. Bennett reports that Kettler has told him, that, should it ever be required to race again, it would be "the work of half an hour" to put it back on the track.

Travis Engen guns his 'clone' R8 into Turn 1 at Sebring, 2010. (Courtesy Martin Spetz)

Engen also competed at the Walter Mitty meeting in 2010.
(Courtesy Martin Spetz)

Andy Wallace, seen here in Jim Roger's 'clone' during 2010, is the only man to have driven an R8 in both contemporary and historic racing. (Courtesy Martin Spetz)

Audi R8 road car and R8 LMS
Honouring the name

By the end of 2010 Audi had become part of Le Mans legend, with nine wins equalling Ferrari's second place total. The circuit of La Sarthe without it had become almost unthinkable. Yet, for almost all of this time, these victories had been marketed to sell a range of, admittedly impressive, saloon and estate – not sports or GT – cars. It did have its TT coupé and roadster, but it could not be thought of as a sports car brand. All this changed in 2007 with the launch of the confusingly, but perhaps fittingly, named R8 – a true, two-seater, mid-engined GT car. Unlike the Le Mans winning R8 after which it was called, this quattro permanent four-wheel-drive car was intended for road use, even if its first born was capable of a top speed of 187mph, hitting 62mph from standstill in 4.6 seconds.

A prototype was shown at the 2003 Frankfurt Motor Show called the Audi 'Le Mans.' The first aluminium monocoque production R8 was revealed at the 2006 Mondial de l'Automobile, Paris, going on sale the following year with a longitudinally-mounted, 4.2-litre V8 engine, and with a 5.2-litre V10 model following at the end of 2008. Audi stated that it mounted the engine as close as possible to the centre of the car in deference to its R8 Le Mans winner, as well as the Auto Union Type C Grand Prix car. In doing so, it achieved a near perfect 44 per cent-front/56 per cent-rear weight distribution, for the best handling balance. It was pointed out that the dry sump engine lubrication was another racing-derived element, enabling the engine to be mounted as close to the road as possible in order to lower the centre of gravity. The car came with six-speed manual transmission, or optional R tronic® sequential shift gearbox with 'shift-by-wire' technology and joystick or paddle control. Also optional was the Audi magnetic ride system, first seen in the TT Coupé.

Fastest of the range, the lighter, 199mph R8 GT, its V10 engine uprated to 560bhp, was first seen in 2010. A Spyder version of the R8, with fully automatic fabric hood, appeared first at the 2009 Frankfurt Motor Show. Initially, this was available with the V10 engine, a V8 becoming available in late 2010.

Having been born out of Audi's racing successes, it was perhaps inevitable that the road-going R8 should become a race car in its own right. The Essen Show, in late November 2008, saw the eagerly awaited unveiling of the R8 LMS, code named at Ingolstadt the R16, and eligible for the FIA's GT3 class. "Racing a road car is a culmination of all we have done since 1999," said Wolfgang Ullrich. "It proves that Audi has made the big step from being seen in touring cars, where we had our last customer programme, to a point where we can compete with Ferrari, Porsche, and Aston Martin. We are now the most sporty brand in the top market segment. I think we can show this with the car that is the top of the Audi programme, the R8, and to make out of this car a customer sport programme. It shows the link between the development of the brand and the development that we have done in motorsport. It was always in our minds that the car would somehow, eventually, get into racing. The R8 road car was born out of racing, so why not bring out a special version of it to take it back to racing?"

Work began on the R8 LMS/R16 in January 2008, with three times DTM champions ABT Sportsline building the first prototype and spearheading the development. This was carried out, as Ullrich observed, "only at the level

An early Audi R8 road car. Given the racing heritage of its namesake, the Paul Ricard circuit setting could be deemed appropriate. (Author's collection)

necessary." Thus, as many existing components were used as possible. It was felt that the lightweight aluminium Audi Space Frame (ASF) used for the road car was a "perfect" basis for motorsport. Neckarsulm-based Audi subsidiary quattro GmbH took a standard R8 production chassis from the line and bolted in a steel roll cage – the wall thickness of which exceeded the regulations – while the Audi Hungaria Kft production line, at Györ, supplied the

5.2-litre FSI direct fuel injection engine, as seen in the 90-degree V10 version of the R8. It was observed that the direct petrol injection was something that Audi had first developed with the original R8 Le Mans winner.

Perhaps the main challenge was to make a rear-wheel drive car out of a four-wheel drive one with a completely different drive train. Four-wheel drive systems, such as the Audi quattro drive, standard on the road-going R8,

The other drivers

In addition to the drivers already profiled, a further 15 raced an Audi R8 (not including the 1999 R8R and R8C) on one or two occasions. Of these, Austrian Philipp Peter was the only one to taste victory, when he shared the winning car at Sebring in 2003 with Frank Biela and Marco Werner. He also drove a factory car, the year before, at Le Mans. Others who raced the R8 twice were Tom Coronel, Jean-Marc Gounon, Hiroki Katoh, Ralf Kelleners, Perry McCarthy, Mika Salo, and Dorsey Schroeder. One-off drives were given to Christian Abt, Yannick Dalmas, Johnny Kane, Michael Krumm, Jan Lammers, Jan Magnussen, Franck Montagny, and Didier Theys.

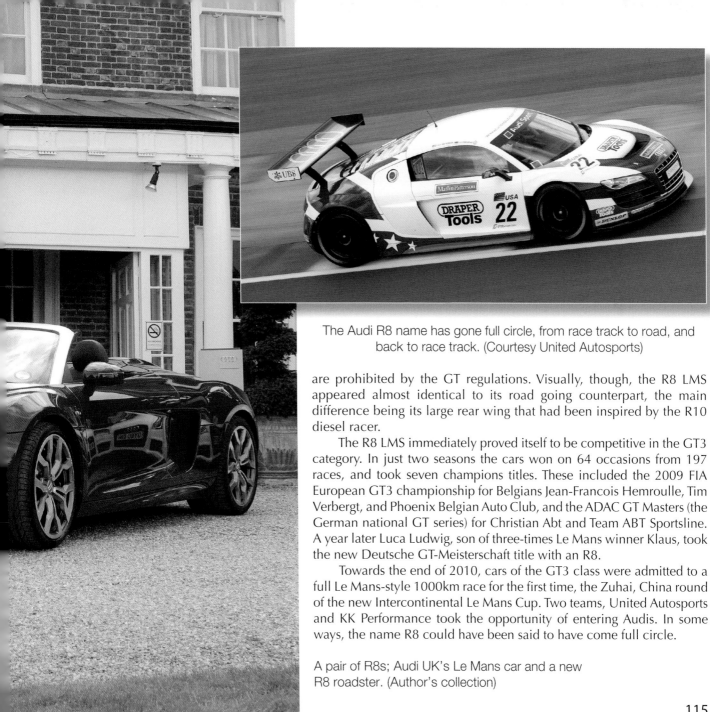

The Audi R8 name has gone full circle, from race track to road, and back to race track. (Courtesy United Autosports)

are prohibited by the GT regulations. Visually, though, the R8 LMS appeared almost identical to its road going counterpart, the main difference being its large rear wing that had been inspired by the R10 diesel racer.

The R8 LMS immediately proved itself to be competitive in the GT3 category. In just two seasons the cars won on 64 occasions from 197 races, and took seven champions titles. These included the 2009 FIA European GT3 championship for Belgians Jean-Francois Hemroulle, Tim Verbergt, and Phoenix Belgian Auto Club, and the ADAC GT Masters (the German national GT series) for Christian Abt and Team ABT Sportsline. A year later Luca Ludwig, son of three-times Le Mans winner Klaus, took the new Deutsche GT-Meisterschaft title with an R8.

Towards the end of 2010, cars of the GT3 class were admitted to a full Le Mans-style 1000km race for the first time, the Zuhai, China round of the new Intercontinental Le Mans Cup. Two teams, United Autosports and KK Performance took the opportunity of entering Audis. In some ways, the name R8 could have been said to have come full circle.

A pair of R8s; Audi UK's Le Mans car and a new
R8 roadster. (Author's collection)

115

Appendix 1 – List of races

R8R and R8C

Date	Event	Drivers	Chassis	Result	Race#
1999					
20/3	Sebring	Alboreto/Capello/Johansson	R8R-205	3rd	77
		McCarthy/Biela/Pirro	R8R-204	5th	78
	Le Mans	Pirro/Biela/Theys	R8R-306	3rd	8
		Alboreto/Capello/Aiello	R8R-307	4th	7
		Johansson/Ortelli/Abt	R8C-102	DNF	9
		Weaver/Wallace/McCarthy	R8C-101	DNF	10
2000					
1/4	Charlotte	Biela/Pirro	R8R-308	6th	78
		Capello/Alboreto/McNish	R8R-306	DNF	77
13/5	Silverstone	Capello/McNish	R8R-306	3rd	77
		Biela/Pirro	R8R-308	4th	78

R8

Date	Event	Drivers	Chassis	Result	Race#
2000					
19/3	Sebring	Biela/Kristensen/Pirro	R8-402	1st	78
		Alboreto/Capello/McNish	R8-403	2nd	77
17-18/6	Le Mans	Biela/Kristensen/Pirro	R8-404	1st	8
		Aiello/McNish/Ortelli	R8-403	2nd	9
		Abt/Alboreto/Capello	R8-402	3rd	7
9/7	Nürburgring	Biela/Pirro	R8-405	3rd	78
		Capello/McNish	R8-403	DNF	77
23/7	Sears Point	Capello/McNish	R8-403	1st	77
		Biela/Pirro	R8-405	2nd	78
6/8	Mosport	Capello/McNish	R8-403	1st	77
		Biela/Pirro	R8-405	17th	78
3/9	Dallas	Biela/Pirro	R8-405	1st	78

Date	Event	Drivers	Chassis	Result	Race#
		Capello/McNish	R8-403	2nd	77
10/9	Portland	Capello/McNish	R8-403	1st	77
		Biela/Pirro	R8-405	4th	78
1/10	Road Atlanta	Alboreto/Capello/McNish	R8-403	1st	77
		Biela/Kristensen/Pirro	R8-405	2nd	78
15/10	Laguna Seca	Capello/McNish	R8-403	1st	77
		Biela/Pirro	R8-405	2nd	78
29/10	Las Vegas	Biela/Pirro	R8-405	1st	78
		Capello/McNish	R8-403	2nd	77
31/12	Adelaide	Capello/McNish	R8-403	1st	77
		Biela/Pirro	R8-405	16th	78
2001					
4/3	Dallas	Capello/Kristensen	R8-502	1st	1
		Biela/Pirro	R8-503	2nd	2
		Wallace/Schroeder	R8-405	4th	38
18/3	Sebring	Aiello/Alboreto/Capello	R8-502	1st	1
		Biela/Kristensen/Pirro	R8-503	2nd	2
		Kelleners/Schroeder/Wallace	R8-405	3rd	38
		Johansson/Smith	R8-403	4th	18
14/4	Donington	Capello/Kristiensen	R8-502	1st	1
		Biela/Pirro	R8-503	2nd	2
		Johansson/Smith	R8-403	3rd	7
20/5	Jarama	Capello/Kristensen	R8-501	1st	1
		Biela/Pirro	R8-503	2nd	2
		Johansson/Smith	R8-403	4th	7
16-17/6	Le Mans	Biela/Kristensen/Pirro	R8-501	1st	1
		Aiello/Capello/Pescatori	R8-505	2nd	2
		Herbert/Kelleners/Theys	R8-502	DNF	3
		Coronel/Johansson/Lemarié	R8-403	DNF	4
15/7	Estoril	Coronel/Johansson/Lemarié	R8-403	DNF	7
22/7	Sears Point	Capello/Kristensen	R8-501	1st	1
		Biela/Pirro	R8-503	2nd	2
		Wallace/Herbert	R8-405	4th	38
5/8	Portland	Biela/Pirro	R8-503	2nd	2
		Herbert/Wallace	R8-405	3rd	38
		Capello/Kristensen	R8-501	5th	1

Date	Event	Drivers	Chassis	Result	Race#
5/8	Most	Johansson/Lemarié	R8-403	1st	7
19/8	Mosport	Biela/Pirro	R8-503	1st	2
		Herbert/Wallace	R8-405	14th	38
		Capello/Kristensen	R8-501	DNF	1
25/8	Mid-Ohio	Capello/Kristensen	R8-505	2nd	1
		Biela/Pirro	R8-503	4th	2
		Herbert/Wallace	R8-405	5th	38
9/9	Laguna Seca	Biela/Pirro	R8-503	1st	2
		Herbert/Wallace	R8-405	2nd	38
		Johansson/Lemarié	R8-403	3rd	18
		Capello/Kristensen	R8-505	DNF	1
6/10	Road Atlanta	Biela/Pirro	R8-503	1st	2
		Johansson/Lemairé	R8-403	2nd	18
		Herbert/Wallace	R8-405	3rd	38
		Capello/Kristensen	R8-505	DNF	1
2002					
17/3	Sebring	Capello/Herbert/Pescatori	R8-602	1st	2
		Johansson/Lammers/Wallace	R8-505	2nd	38
		Biela/Kristensen/Pirro	R8-601	5th	1
19/5	Sears Point	Herbert/Kristensen	R8-505	2nd	38
		Biela/Capello/Pirro	R8-405	15th	1
15-16/6	Le Mans	Biela/Kristensen/Pirro	R8-601	1st	1
		Capello/Herbert/Pescatori	R8-602	2nd	2
		Krumm/Peter/Werner	R8-603	3rd	3
		Ara/Dalmaas/Katoh	R8-501	7th	5
30/6	Mid-Ohio	Pirro/Biela	R8-601	1st	1
		Capello/Kristensen	R8-602	2nd	2
		Herbert/Johansson	R8-505	10th	38
17/7	Road America	Capello/Kristensen	R8-602	1st	2
		Pirro/Biela	R8-601	2nd	1
		Herbert/Johansson	R8-505	3rd	38
21/7	Washington	Capello/Kristensen	R8-602	2nd	2
		Biela/Pirro	R8-601	3rd	1
		Herbert/Johansson	R8-505	5th	38
3/8	Trois-Rivières	Capello/Kristensen	R8-602	1st	2
		Biela/Pirro	R8-601	2nd	1

Date	Event	Drivers	Chassis	Result	Race#
		Herbert/Johansson	R8-505	3rd	38
18/8	Mosport	Capello/Kristensen	R8-602	1st	2
		Herbert/Johansson	R8-505	2nd	38
		Biela/Pirro	R8-601	DNF	1
24/8	Suzuka	Ara/Katoh	R8-501	DNF	61
22/9	Laguna Seca	Biela/Pirro	R8-601	1st	1
		Herbert/Johansson	R8-505	2nd	38
		Capello/Kristensen	R8-602	4th	2
5/10	Miami	Biela/Pirro	R8-601	1st	1
		Capello/Kristensen	R8-602	3rd	2
		Herbert/Johansson	R8-505	5th	38
12/10	Road Atlanta	Capello/Kristensen	R8-602	1st	2
		Herbert/Johansson	R8-505	2nd	38
		Biela/Pirro	R8-601	6th	1

2003

Date	Event	Drivers	Chassis	Result	Race#
15/3	Sebring	Biela/Peter/Werner	R8-604	1st	1
		Johansson/Lehto/Peter	R8-505	2nd	38
		Kane/McNarthy/Salo	R8-603	6th	9
14-15/6	Le Mans	Johansson/Lehto/Pirro	R8-505	3rd	6
		Ara/Magnussen/Werner	R8-602	4th	5
		Biela/McCarthy/Salo	R8-603	DNF	10
29/6	Road Atlanta	Herbert/Lehto	R8-505	1st	38
		Biela/Werner	R8-604	2nd	1
27/7	Sears Point	Biela/Werner	R8-604	2nd	1
		Herbert/Lehto	R8-505	3rd	38
3/8	Trois Rivières	Biela/Werner	R8-604	1st	1
		Herbert/Lehto	R8-505	2nd	38
17/8	Mosport	Biela/Werner	R8-604	1st	1
		Herbert/Lehto	R8-505	20th	38
24/8	Road America	Herbert/Lehto	R8-505	1st	38
		Biela/Werner	R8-604	7th	1
31/8	Spa-Francorchamps	Ara/Kristensen	R8-601	1st	25
7/9	Laguna Seca	Biela/Werner	R8-604	1st	1
		Herbert/Lehto	R8-505	4th	38
27/9	Miami	Herbert/Lehto	R8-505	1st	38
		Biela/Werner	R8-604	2nd	1

Date	Event	Drivers	Chassis	Result	Race#
18/10	Road Atlanta	Herbert/Lehto	R8-505	1st	38
		Biela/Werner	R8-604	3rd	1
9/11	Le Mans	Ara/Kristensen	R8-602	1st	5
2004					
20/3	Sebring	Biela/Kaffer/McNish	R8-603	1st	28
		Lehto/Pirro/Werner	R8-505	2nd	38
		Davies/Herbert/Smith	R8-604	3rd	88
9/5	Monza	Davies/Herbert	R8-604	1st	88
		Kaffer/McNish	R8-603	2nd	8
		Ara/Capello/Kristensen	R8-602	3rd	5
12-13/6	Le Mans	Ara/Capello/Kristensen	R8-602	1st	5
		Davies/Herbert/Smith	R8-604	2nd	88
		Lehto/Werner/Pirro	R8-505	3rd	2
		Biela/Kaffer/McNish	R8-603	5th	8
27/6	Mid-Ohio	Lehto/Werner	R8-505	1st	38
3/7	Nürburgring	Kaffer/McNish	R8-603	1st	8
		Davies/Herbert	R8-604	2nd	88
		Ara/Capello	R8-602	5th	5
5/7	Lime Rock	Lehto/Werner	R8-505	1st	38
18/7	Sears Point	Lehto/Werner	R8-505	1st	38
25/7	Portland	Lehto/Werner	R8-505	1st	38
8/8	Mosport	Lehto/Werner	R8-505	2nd	38
14/8	Silverstone	Kaffer/McNish	R8-603	1st	8
		Ara/Capello	R8-602	2nd	5
		Davies/Herbert	R8-604	3rd	88
22/8	Road America	Lehto/Werner	R8-505	1st	38
11/9	Spa-Francorchamps	Davies/Herbert	R8-604	1st	88
		Ara/Capello	R8-602	2nd	5
		Kaffer/McNish	R8-603	DNF	8
25/9	Road Atlanta	Lehto/Werner	R8-505	1st	38
		Herbert/Kaffer	R8-605	2nd	2
17/10	Laguna Seca	Herbert/Kaffer	R8-605	1st	2
		Lehto/Werner	R8-505	2nd	38
2005					
19/3	Sebring	Kristiansen/Lehto/Werner	R8-605	1st	1

Date	Event	Drivers	Chassis	Result	Race#
		Biela/McNish/Pirro	R8-505	2nd	2
17/4	Road Atlanta	Lehto/Werner	R8-605	1st	1
		Biela/Pirro	R8-505	3rd	2
17/4	Spa-Francorchamps	Guonon/Ortelli	R8-603	DNF	4
22/5	Mid-Ohio	Biela/Pirro	R8-505	3rd	2
		Lehto/Werner	R8-605	18th	1
18-19/6	Le Mans	Kristensen/Lehto/Werner	R8-605	1st	3
		Biela/McNish/Pirro	R8-505	3rd	2
		Gounon/Montagny/Ortelli	R8-603	4th	4
4/7	Lime Rock	Lehto/Werner	R8-605	1st	1
		Biela/Pirro	R8-505	2nd	2
17/7	Sears Point	Biela/Pirro	R8-505	1st	2
		Lehto/Werner	R8-605	3rd	1
30/7	Portland	Biela/Pirro	R8-505	1st	2
		Lehto/Werner	R8-605	DNF	1
13/8	Silverstone	McNish/Ortelli	R8-603	1st	4
21/8	Road America	Biela/Pirro	R8-605	1st	2
		Lehto/Werner	R8-505	3rd	1
4/9	Nürburgring	McNish/Ortelli	R8-603	2nd	4
4/9	Mosport	Lehto/Werner	R8-605	2nd	1
		Biela/Pirro	R8-505	3rd	2
1/10	Road Atlanta	Biela/Pirro	R8-505	1st	2
		Lehto/Werner	R8-605	7th	1
15/10	Laguna Seca	Biela/Pirro	R8-505	2nd	2
		Lehto/Werner	R8-605	4th	1
13/11	Istanbul	McNish/Ortelli	R8-603	2nd	4
2006					
13/5	Houston	Capello/McNish	R8-605	1st	2
21/5	Mid-Ohio	Capello/McNish	R8-605	3rd	2
1/7	Lime Rock	Capello/McNish	R8-605	1st	2

Appendix 2 – The cars

R8-401 – A test car for Audi Sport that remains in the possession of Audi.

R8-402 – Competed in two races before becoming a show car. The first R8 to win a race, the 2000 12 Hours of Sebring.

R8-403 – A particularly successful car that took the 2000 ALMS championship as well as seven victories. Appeared in 'crocodile' livery at Adelaide, before being sold to Phil Bennett and raced by Stefan Johnasson in Gulf colours. Later purchased by Aaron Hsu for 'historic' racing, and then Joe Graziano, before being sold to the ROFGO Collection.

R8-404 – One race, one win. The 2000 Le Mans victor was retired to the Audi museum in Ingolstadt.

R8-405 – A factory car in the 2000 ALMS following Le Mans, this was sold to Champion Racing for the following year. Despite being raced on 18 occasions it achieved only two victories. Subsequently purchased by Jim Rogers for 'historic' racing.

R8-406 – Never raced show car.

R8-501 – The first of the second generation 2001 cars, this was a test car that raced just once when the TFSI engine made its debut at Jarama. It then competed at Le Mans and in three ALMS races, all bearing the number one, before being damaged at Mosport, repaired, and sold to Team Goh, which entered it twice the following year. Subsequently sold to Aaron Hsu and then to George Stauffer.

R8-502 – This won the first three of its five races, including Sebring 2001, and was then used by Champion for Le Mans.

R8-503 – The winning car at Le Mans in 2001, as well as Biela and Pirro's drive that year in the ALMS. Four victories was its total from 11 starts.

R8-504 – Never raced.

R8-505 – The most raced and successful of all R8s with a total of 15 victories from 47 starts. Capello and Kristensen's 2001 car for the ALMS. Then entered by Champion over four seasons, taking the 2004 ALMS title. Acquired by RM Motorsports in 2006 and never raced since.

R8-601 – The 2002 Le Mans winning car, as well as a regular in the ALMS that year. Loaned by Audi to the Le Mans museum in 2004, having won a total of four races.

R8-602 – Kristensen's mount for the 2002 ALMS title. Taken over by Team Goh in 2003 and won Le Mans a year later. Eight wins from 18 starts, making it the second most successful of the R8s.

R8-603 – Third factory car at Le Mans in 2002. Bought by Audi UK for two subsequent attempts at Le Mans, Sebring 2003, and the 2004 LMS. Loaned to ORECA for its fourth Le Mans, in 2005, and another year in the LMS. Still owned by Audi UK. A four times winner.

R8-604 – A 2002 car rebuilt in the winter of 2002/2003 by

Team Joest for the ALMS. Raced by Team Veloqx as a sister car to R8-603 for the 2004 Le Mans and LMS, winning the latter. Scored the R8's 50th victory at Spa that year, one of six wins for this chassis. Still owned by Sam Li.

R8-605 – Last of the factory-built R8s, built in 2002, but not making its race debut until 2004. Used by Team Champion to win that year's Le Mans and ALMS. Was used for the 2006 'Farewell Tour.' Owned by Audi North America.

R8-606 – 'Clone' car built from parts by Champion Racing in 2005. Initially purchased by Tom Gonzales for a museum in Reno, and sold to Travis Engen for 'historic' racing.

R8-607 – 'Clone' car built from parts by Kettler Motor Werks in 2009, and purchased by Jim Rogers for 'historic' racing.

Team Goh's R8 heads out of Indianapolis for Arnage, as night falls at Le Mans. (Author's collection)

Also from Veloce Publishing ...

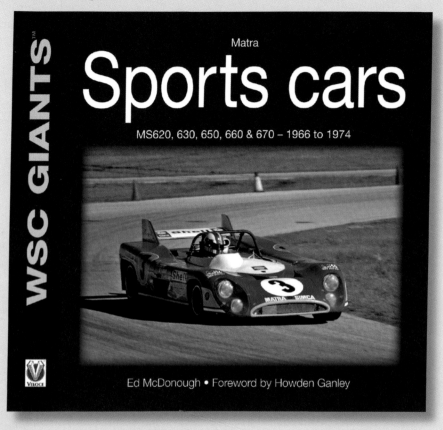

The late 1960s and early 1970s were a significant era in the world of international sports car racing. Porsche vs Ferrari vs Alfa Romeo vs Matra provided some of the best racing for sports cars ever witnessed, and by 1973, the Matra prototype – little more than a Grand Prix car with full bodywork – was dominating the scene. This is the story of a great time, and a great model, in motorsport.

Paperback • 21x19.5cm • £15.99 • 128 pages • 106 colour & b&w pictures • ISBN: 978-1-845842-61-1

* Prices subject to change • P&P extra • visit www.veloce.co.uk for more information
email sales@veloce.co.uk tel +44 (0) 1305 260068

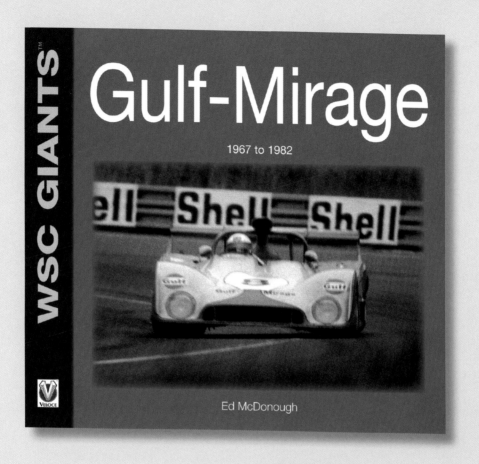

WSC GIANTS™

Gulf-Mirage

1967 to 1982

Ed McDonough

Details the origin and history of the Mirage sports cars, designed by the British-based John Wyer Automotive firm to contest the various versions of the World Sports Car Championship between 1967 and 1975, funded by the Gulf Oil Corporation. The cars began as developments of the Ford GT40, but they soon assumed their own identity. This book includes the developmental and race history, with a full list of all events and individual chassis numbers.

Paperback • 21x19.5cm • £15.99 • 128 pages • 100 colour & b&w pictures • ISBN: 978-1-845842-51-2

* Prices subject to change • P&P extra • visit www.veloce.co.uk for more information
email sales@veloce.co.uk tel +44 (0) 1305 260068

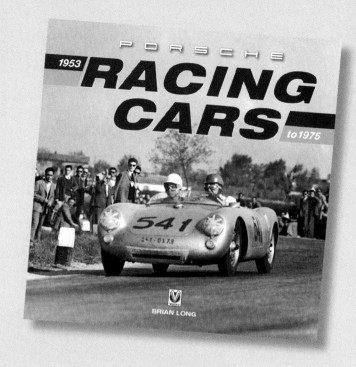
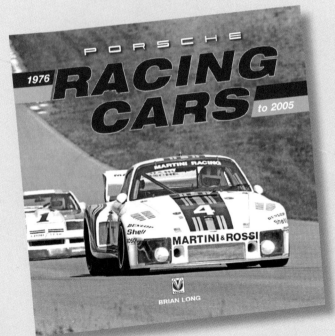

Index